Messiah REVEALED
in the PASSOVER
פסח

by

Hannah Nesher

Scripture quotations are taken from the Hebrew-English Bible. Copyright © by Bible Society in Israel 1996 and the Israel Association for the Dissemination of Biblical Writings. The Bible Society in Israel, P.O. Box 44 Jerusalem, 91000 Israel

Scripture quotations taken from the HOLY BIBLE, NEW INTERNATIONAL VERSION. Copyright © 1973, 1978, 1984 by International Bible Society. Used by permission of Zondervan Publishing House.

ISBN# 978-0-9733892-6-5

For speaking engagements please contact Hannah:

Hannah Nesher, Voice for Israel
Suite #313- 11007 Jasper Ave.
Edmonton, Alberta
T5K 0K6 Canada

www.voiceforisrael.net

Copyright © 2014 by Voice for Israel

All rights reserved under International Copyright Law. Contents and/or cover may not be reproduced in whole or in part in any form without the express written consent of the Publisher.

Cover design by James Vanderwekken - jvnderwe@hotmail.com
Cover illustration by Peter Jones - www.messianicway.com

Publication assistance and
digital printing in Canada by

pagemaster.ca

DEDICATION

To the God of my fathers, Avraham, Yitzchak and Yaacov,

יהוה
אהיה אשר אהיה

To You whose name says

You will be whoever You will be –

Thanks for being all I have ever needed!

And to Your Son and Messiah Y'shuah

ישוע

For your obedience to the Father

For being led like a lamb to the slaughter

For pouring out your soul unto death

So that I could live!

A Special Thank You

I would like to say *todah rabah* (thanks very much) and publicly acknowledge my debt of gratitude towards all the people who helped with this work.

First of all, to my mother and father who gave me life. Thank you for your courage in training up this daughter of yours through all our ups and downs. Although we may not always agree on theology, your love has remained constant.

To my friend and intercessor, Marilyn, thank you for your fervent prayers and moral support - as well as the hours you spent proofreading my writing. Thanks also to Radek, Juliett & Nadia.

To my children, Clayton, Courtney, Timothy, Liat, and Avi-ad, who each supplied material and inspiration for my writing. Thank you for your patience with the crazy times in our family - for loving and forgiving me whenever I messed up (which was often). I love you!

To all our ministry partners for your faithful love, fervent prayers and generous support. May you be fully rewarded by the God of Israel under whose wings you have taken refuge! (Ruth 2:12)

To James Vanderwekken for his awesome graphic design work and technical support.   L'hatzlachah ! (to your success !)

To Denis Vanderwekken & his late wife, Corrie for their friendship, support, and help in the journey.   Corrie - I miss you!

I love and appreciate all of you!

Most of all, to the Holy Spirit (Ruach Hakodesh), for granting me the inspiration, motivation, and words to write.

Todah rabah! (thank so very much) תודה רבה

Contents

Note from the Author..9
Introduction..13

PART ONE: IN THE BEGINNING

1   **Beginning of Months**..19

2   **Festival of Liberation**..21
        Setting the Elephants Free.......................................22
        Liberty to the Captives...23
        Freed for What?...25

3   **Birth of a Kingdom of Priests (Cohanim)**............26
        Mount Sinai...27
        Bodies in the Wilderness..28
        Complaint Department..29
        Beware of Discouragement.....................................30
        The Cure...31
        Salvation Not Enough...33

4   **Covenant**..34
        Covenant of Promise Not Annulled by the Law.........36

5   **The Prophetic Meaning of Passover**....................39
        The Lion of Judah Defends Jerusalem.....................39
        Fury Poured Out Again...40
        A Greater Passover...41

6	**Let All Your Males Be Circumcized**..................**44**	
	A Bridegroom of Blood..46	
	Spirit Not Letter..47	
	The Final Verdict..48	
	Yeshua's Circumcision..49	
	Keeping the Commandments is What Matters.............49	
	Circumcision of the Heart......................................50	
7	**Passover: A Season for Harvest**......................**52**	
	The Master Craftsman...53	
	The Seeker...54	
8	**The Feasts of יהוה**..**55**	
	One Law (Torah) and One Custom..............................56	
	Let the Little Children Come Unto Me.........................57	
	The Lamb of God..58	
	Generational Evangelism.......................................58	
	Shadow and Substance..59	
9	**Parallel Images**..**62**	
	Choose a Lamb..62	
	A Lamb for a Household..63	
	A Lamb Without Blemish......................................64	
	A Lamb that was Slain..65	
	He Opened Not His Mouth.....................................66	
	Crucify Him!..67	
10	**Messianic Prophecies Fulfilled in Yeshua**..........**68**	
	Eli, Eli, Lamah Azavtani?......................................69	
	I Will Never Leave Nor Forsake You.......................69	
	Vinegar to Drink...70	
	It is Finished..70	
	The Veil Has Been Torn...71	

	Not a Broken Bone..72
	A Bone of Contention..72
	Isaiah 53: The Controversy..75
11	**The Blood**..**78**
	Obedience Rather than Sacrifice................................79
	And You Shall Apply It...81
	Staying Under the Blood...82
	Doorway of Life..83
	Not Appointed to Wrath..84
	The Coming Lion of Judah.......................................85
	The Fate of the Gentile Believers in the Nations.......86
	A Refuge..87
12	**Preparing for Passover**..**88**
	Spring Cleaning..89
	Traditional Custom vs. Biblical Command...............89
	Cleaning the Chametz...92
	The Candle and the Feather......................................93
	Boasting Against the Branches.................................96
	The Sin of Ingratitude...97
	Without Love We Are Nothing.................................98
	Better Check Your Pews...100

PART TWO: THE SEDER

13	**Preparing for the Seder**....................................**105**
	The Hagaddah...105
	Who to Invite?..106
	The Seder Plate...108
	Elements of the Seder Plate....................................109
	Other Elements on the Seder Table........................111
14	**Order of the Seder**...**114**
	We Light the Candles...115

    The First Cup of Wine (Kiddush) 115
    Urchatz - We Wash 117
    Karpas - Parsely 117
    Matzah 118
    Yachatz 119
    Marror - The Bitter Herbs 120
    Charoset 121
    Mah Nishtanah 121
    Magid - Tell the Story of Passover 122
    The Second Cup of Wine (Eser Makot) 124
    Pesach - The Lamb 128
    Shulchan Corech - The Festive Meal 130
    The Third Cup of Redemption & the Afikomen 130
    The Fourth Cup and Hallel (Praise) 135
    Next Year in Jerusalem 135

15   What About Easter? 137
    The Development of Easter 138
    We Will Not Listen! 140
    A Festival to the Lord 141
    Do Not Worship Me in 'Their' (Pagan) Ways 142
    Devised in His Own Heart 144
    God is Judge 145
    Bowing in the House of Rimmon 147
    Falling Away 148

16   A Call to Passover 150

17   Final Prayer 153

Appendix 154

Note From The Author

This book has taken several years to complete. Why, I wonder, has it taken so long? Perhaps it is because this one is so crucial, especially for Jewish people. It deals with the very foundation of our faith – salvation through the Passover Lamb. As Messianic Jews, we see Yeshua (Jesus) the Messiah as the fulfillment of this wondrous event. The Exodus has now been made popular by the hit movie and video, Prince of Egypt, (which we have probably watched over a hundred times with our youngest daughter). So many people are familiar with the basic story; and yet there exists a message that goes so much deeper than what appears on the surface. I feel a bit like a woman at the end of her labor, just before the last stage of giving birth. Any woman who has been in labor knows this difficult period in which you feel like it's gone on more than long enough and you just want it to be over, but you know you have to go through it until the end. Any labor coach or spouse who has accompanied a woman through the process of labor and delivery can probably testify to this difficult time. And those who haven't been through it or witnessed anyone else perform such an amazing feat as giving birth will just have to take my word for it – it's tough! At the time of this writing, I am pregnant (again) and so these things are being refreshed in my consciousness. I am also struggling with fatigue, morning sickness that lasts until around 6:00 P.M., and raging hormones – not to mention a two-year old who needs constant supervision. Her motto is, *"If I'm quiet, you'd better come and find me!"* But the Holy Spirit gave me a Word to complete what I had started:

> **"And in this I give advice: It is to your advantage not only to be doing what you began and were desiring to do a year ago; but now you also must complete the doing of it; that as there was a readiness to desire it, so there also may be a completion out of what you have."** (2 Corinthians 8:10-11)

Some projects are fun and exciting to start, but to carry them through to completion when the emotion has worn off requires perseverance and endurance. I'm sure that marathon runners or athletes of any kind (of which I am definitely not one) can relate. We must press on to run the race with perseverance to the finish line to win the prize. "...**let us run with endurance the race that is set before us**." (Hebrews 12:1) That goes for all of us!

It has been my goal throughout these books to share my experiences and background as an Orthodox Jewish girl who came to faith in Yeshua (Jesus) as my Messiah and Savior, in order to bring light and truth to both the Jewish and Christian communities. As Messianic Jews, we hope to act as a bridge between the two groups, with the ability to reach out in both directions. '*In the middle*' is not always an easy or comfortable place to be, especially when those you are standing between are often feuding with one another. One tends to take pot shots to the head occasionally in the crossfire. My brother wrote to me once about his disillusionment with life, with religion, and religious hypocrites. And then he wrote, "*Your videos are very interesting, but I still can't get the connection between Judaism and Christianity.*" There are, I suspect, many people, both Jewish and Christian, who still 'just don't get it'.

I once had an interesting experience that made this incongruity between Christianity and Judaism even more real to me. A Christian group organized a repentance conference held in

Jerusalem. Its purpose was to express deep regret and remorse over the sins of Christians over the span of history towards the Jewish people. When I approached the doorway, a sweet looking woman wearing a name tag asked me where I wished to be seated – with the Jewish people who had come to receive the plea for forgiveness or with the Christians who had come to repent for the atrocities committed by them against Jews. Which side indeed? It had been a long time since I had felt that I must choose sides. In the end, we found the solution – obviously others had also experienced this dilemma and so a third section had formed on its own – the Messianic Jews.

Except for these rare occasions, I now feel at home with both my Jewish heritage and my faith in Yeshua. I hope others will as well. The reconciling of my identity crisis did not take place immediately; it has been a journey with the Good Shepherd leading every step of the way. It is my hope and prayer that others will also find peace and rest for their souls in Him. Just as teachers in the 'little red schoolhouse' faced the peculiar challenge of trying to reach and interest all levels from K to graduation, I have also attempted to teach all levels simultaneously. This reminds me a little of my days as an ESL (English as a Second Language) teacher in Bible College. Students in the same class ranged all the way from absolutely illiterate, even in their own language, to almost fluent in English. And yet we all had fun together that semester; we learned new things and formed bonds of friendship across the miles of language, culture, and generation. And so I hope that those of you more advanced in your study of the Feasts and your roots will have patience with those just beginning. And those just beginning will not tear their hair out, please, with concepts that fly over your head (for now).

May Jewish individuals, as well as those of other faiths reading this book come to the wondrous realization that Yeshua (Jesus) is our Passover Lamb, and find salvation in Him. It is not an accident or coincidence that this book has come into your hands, but a divine appointment! For the many Christians seeking a deeper richness in faith and intimacy in walking with the Lord, I hope that this study of the Passover will bring new and wonderful things in God's word to light. To God be all the glory!

Happy Passover! May yours be a joyous and meaningful celebration.

Introduction

For over thirty years, I celebrated Passover at a traditional Jewish family service and meal called a Seder, which literally means, 'order' in Hebrew. Every evening before the festival, we would search for any hidden chametz (crumbs of leavened bread) by following after my father, holding a candle and feather, sweeping each crumb discovered with cries of delight by the children into a dustpan, later to be burned outside the home. Each year, I sang, along with the others at the Seder table about Eliyahu Hanavi (Elijah the Prophet) who would come with 'Moshiach Ben David' (Messiah son of David). We would actually set a place for Eliyahu at the table, and at one point in the Seder, open the door, as if perchance this year he may be waiting to enter – signifying the Jewish longing each year for Messiah. At every Seder table we retold, as commanded, the story of the deliverance of our forefathers from slavery in Egypt and how the Israelites were saved from the angel of death by placing the blood of the lamb on their doorposts. We always ended the Seder in sleepy contentment, satisfied to the full with an abundance of food and four cups of wine, with the refrain, L'shana Haba'ah b'Yirushalayim (Next year in Jerusalem). Never once did I question any of the spiritual significance of these traditions, scriptures, or songs. I never wondered why we had to rid our home of yeast, or who this Messiah was, or how the blood of an innocent lamb had saved our ancestors? My heart contained within it no yearning to leave my home and family to celebrate Passover the next year in Jerusalem. The Seder existed simply as another Orthodox Jewish family ritual that I considered something to be endured in order to keep peace in the family, rather than a meaningful spiritual experience.

Then one day, something marvelous happened. God heard the pitiful cries of one of His sheep; He had compassion on this lost lamb and sent someone to deliver a message to me. It was this: "Jesus loves you. He will never leave you and never forsake you." With the power of this two-edged sword, which is the Word of God, I was delivered from slavery to Satan and the kingdom of darkness through the blood of the Passover lamb, Yeshua Hamashiach (Jesus the Messiah), and entered the Kingdom of Light. I began to read our own Hebrew scriptures and to learn from God's word, the Torah, His instructions for happiness, health, and prosperity through living a holy life that is pleasing to Him. I immersed in the waters of the Mikvah[1], and emerged, as if on the other side of the Sea of Reeds,[2] free! With a new heart, the Ruach HaKodesh (Holy Spirit) filled my being and compelled me to walk in God's ways and keep His commandments.[3] Things began to fall into place, to make sense; my life gained purpose, meaning, and order. Suddenly, the Passover took on incredible significance for me to remember, not only the salvation of our people from Egypt so long ago, but also my own salvation through the broken body and shed blood of my Messiah.

A Temporary Blindness

How could I have celebrated Passover so many years without understanding its central meaning? How could I not have seen the blood of the lamb as a foreshadow of the Lamb of God who was slain for the salvation of all Mankind? There are many reasons,

---

[1] Ritual water immersion, usually called 'baptism' in Christian terminology.
[2] The name of the body of water the Israelites passed through is *Yam Soof*, which is translated *'Sea of Reeds'*, not Red Sea.
[3] Ezekiel 36:27

but the main one is that which holds true for most Jewish people. It is a divine hand that put a temporary blindness over the eyes of most Jewish people with regards to seeing or understanding our own Messiah. Why would He do this? The scriptures make known this mystery: blindness in part happened to the Jewish people in order that the fullness of the Gentiles would be harvested into the kingdom. The apostle, Paul, warned the non-Jewish followers of Yeshua not to be ignorant of this,

> **"For I do not desire, brethren, that you should be ignorant of this mystery, lest you should be wise in your own opinion, that blindness in part has happened to Israel until the fullness of the Gentiles has come in."** (Rom. 11:25)

Ignorance of the fact that this 'blindness in part' happened to Israel within the perfect plan of God, to bring about His purposes of gathering non-Jews into the Kingdom, has resulted in exactly what Paul warned against – conceit and arrogance. This pride - exactly the same sin that trapped satan and condemned him and his fallen angels forever to the lake of fire - is what has snared some within the Christian Church. It has caused them to commit abominable acts of torture and persecution, and has resulted in the extermination of millions of Jewish people over the centuries for this very blindness towards the Messiah that actually made it possible for them to enter the Kingdom of God. Isn't this ludicrous? Paul gave a stern warning to non-Jewish Believers:

> **"Do not be haughty, but fear. For if God did not spare the natural branches, He may not spare you either."** (Rom. 11:20-21)

Keeping the Feast

It is for this reason that all of us, whether Jew or Gentile, need to heed both the commandments of our God in the Old Testament (Tanach) and the exhortation of the apostle Paul in the New to 'keep the feast.'

> **"Therefore let us keep the feast, not with old leaven, nor with the leaven of malice and wickedness, but with the unleavened bread of sincerity and truth."**
> (1 Cor. 5:8)

We all need to cleanse not only our homes, but also our hearts, of any chametz, any leaven, a symbol of sin and especially pride.

Passover is not temporary but forever.

> **"So this day shall be to you a memorial; and you shall keep it as a feast to the Lord throughout your generations. You shall keep it as a feast as an everlasting ordinance."** (Ex. 12:14)

Everlasting is a very long time. But we may celebrate the Passover each year– not in bored resignation at the necessity of keeping an empty religious ritual – but in full realization of the spiritual significance of the festival.

PART ONE

IN THE BEGINNING

CHAPTER ONE

BEGINNING OF MONTHS

Passover is actually the beginning of the Biblical calendar year.

> **"This month shall be your beginning of months; it shall be the first month of the year to you."** (Exodus 12:2)

For those who thought the Jewish New Year (Rosh Hashana) takes place in the fall of the year, welcome to the difference between today's rabbinical form of Judaism and Biblical truth! The Jewish people picked up many pagan customs and traditions from their period of Babylonian exile. These changes, including the naming of some Hebrew months after Babylonian gods (Tammuz, etc) have been incorporated into modern day Judaism. It is the Babylonian calendar that begins its new year in the fall (the seventh month of Tishrei), whereas God has instructed us to start our new year in the spring on the first of Aviv (now called Nissan)[1], which is at the season of Passover. So for anyone who wishes you a happy New Year in September or even January 1st, you can tell them that they've missed it, 'cause the authentic

---

1 Biblically, the month of Nissan is called Aviv. During Israel's Babylonian exile, several Hebrew names for the months were exchanged for their Babylonian counterparts and include the names of pagan gods such as Tamuz.

Biblical New Year is celebrated at Pesach time!

Passover, the 'Spring Feast' represents new beginnings. As the cold death of winter makes way for the gentle warmth and light of spring, we tend to walk outside more and may discover the stirrings of new life. As we notice tiny green leaves appearing on previously bare branches and trees filled to overflowing with pink and violet blossoms, we can't help but feel renewed in our spirits. Even those suffering depression and heaviness may feel it lift at the beginning of spring. Passover brings hope of a fresh start, another chance to try again, even if the season of winter has seemed hard and bitter. Passover represents the new life we have in Messiah.[2]

> **"Therefore, if anyone is in Messiah, he is a new creation; old things have passed away; behold, all things have become new."** (2 Cor. 5:17)

---

[2] *Note:* Even those living in the Southern Hemisphere can appreciate the spiritual significance of 'new life' at this time of year.

CHAPTER TWO

FESTIVAL OF LIBERATION

We understand Passover to be a celebration of the Israelites' liberation from slavery in Egypt. When we celebrate the Passover, however, we are to consider it not just 'their' liberation, but also a declaration of our own personal freedom. Egypt can represent much more than a place on the map. In Hebrew, the word for Egypt, 'Mitzrayim', shares the same root with the word for boundaries or limitations. Each of us has been bound to some extent by fears, by doubts about our abilities by others' opinions of our worth, and by past abuse or failure. We may see ourselves, as did the ten Israelite spies, as mere 'grasshoppers' in our own eyes and think we could never accomplish anything for God. We may restrict ourselves with our own lingering 'slave mentality', or live in bondage to selfishness, greed, lust or addictions. Passover is the season of liberation! It is a time for breakthrough – to break out of our own personal *'Mitzrayim'* – to transcend the boundaries or limitations that others or our own faulty thinking patterns have held us captive and to be released into the fullness of God's purpose for our lives. Halleluyah! I sense an excitement in the spirit; an anticipation of a new freedom that we could not even have imagined existed!

> "Now the Lord (Ha-Adon) is the Spirit (Ruach); and where the Spirit of the Lord is, there is liberty." (2 Corinthians 3:17)

God doesn't want us walking around dragging our feet, hands hanging limp, heads bowed in shame, looking as if someone's been standing over us with a whip all our lives. He doesn't want us to feel as if we've been stomping in the muck and mire all day, building bricks for the Egyptians' pyramids! Yeshua said that He came to give us life and life more abundantly! (John 10:10) The enemy is the one who has come to steal, kill and destroy. He wants to keep us in bondage, in misery, in defeat. But we must rise up as children of freedom, of the living God, and declare our liberty in Messiah!

Setting the Elephants Free

A story is told of an elephant that had its leg tied to a post since it had joined the circus as a baby. The elephant learned that it could walk only so far and no further. After a period of time, it was no longer necessary to tie the elephant's leg to the post. Even once set free, it would not walk past the previously established limits. We are sometimes like that elephant. Yeshua has paid the price for us to be set free from sin and all bondages of the powers of darkness, but we sometimes refuse to believe it and to embrace the liberty that is our heritage as the redeemed of the Lord. Let us believe by faith that he or she who the Son has set free is free indeed. (John 8:36) In order to live out this freedom however, we must first be transformed in our minds.

Just as the elephants' feet had worn deep grooves in the earth by tramping down the same path day after day, so too do we carve out neural 'grooves' in our mind, by thinking the same thought patterns day in and day out. I received a revelation on this one day while watching a science program about the neural and physiological development of babies. The film showed that in order for a baby to learn new behaviors such as smiling, turning over, or grabbing a toy, their brains must actually develop new neural patterns that accommodate this new behavior. It was one of those 'aha' moments. The scripture about being transformed by the renewing of my mind suddenly took on new meaning.

> **"And do not be conformed to this world, but be transformed by the renewing of your minds, that you may prove what is that good and acceptable and perfect will of God."** (Rom. 12:2)

In order to 'get out of the rut' that I had already worn down in my brain by thinking the same dumb things over and over again, I needed to actually and consciously think new thoughts; to create new neural pathways in my brain – to blaze a new trail in a sense! Where I had previously thought what I felt in my emotions, for example, "I can't", I must now begin to think instead and speak the Word of God, *"I can do all things through the Messiah who strengthens me."* This is not as easy as it sounds. Do you think it's easy to budge an elephant? It's much more comfortable and familiar to walk along the same old paths that we have trodden down for years. But in order to enjoy the freedom that our Messiah died for, we must venture beyond the known into the unknown, full of courage and trust in a God who promises to never leave and never forsake us!

Liberty to the Captives

The slaughter of the Passover lamb brought the Israelites physical deliverance from their Egyptian captivity, but there is an equally painful and real spiritual captivity that we all experience. Our own sins and iniquities trap us and bind us as a strong cord:

> "His own iniquities entrap the wicked man, and he
> is caught in the cords of his sin." (Prov. 5:22)

But Yeshua's mission on earth was to set the captives free:

> "The Spirit of the Lord God is upon Me, Because
> the Lord has anointed Me
> To preach good tidings to the poor;
> He has sent Me to heal
> the brokenhearted,
> To proclaim liberty to the captives,
> And the opening of the prison to
> those who are bound..." (Is. 61:1)

Yeshua, reading these verses from the haftorah portion[1] in the Synagogue one Shabbat, boldly declared Himself to be the fulfillment of these scriptures (Luke 4:16-21).

One of the most heart-wrenching moments of my life happened one Passover when my mother, near collapse under the strain of all the stringent Orthodox Jewish requirements for the preparation of Passover, fell into my arms and cried, *"I'm afraid I will die like this."* And yet she, like most Jewish people, is so afraid of hearing anything about Yeshua (Jesus). Please join me in praying for salvation, not only for my mother, but also for all our loved ones like her, who are afraid they will die in their sins.

> "For if you do not believe that I am He, you will die
> in your sins." (John 8:24)

When they come to the knowledge of the truth of their Messiah, the truth will set them free. (John 8:32)

---

[1] The weekly Sabbath scripture portion read from the prophets.

Freed For What?

Now that we have peeked out and found to our amazement that the prison doors are open, we may ask what the purpose of our freedom is. What, exactly, are we set free to do? We are freed to serve the living God; to become the set apart, holy people that He has destined for us to be. Many people think of the 'law' as a negative thing – a set of restrictions. But lawlessness is anarchy; we need practical instruction and direction in how to live our lives. True liberty is found in living according to the Word of God in the Torah.

> **"So shall I keep Your law (Torah) continually, forever and ever. And I will walk at liberty, for I seek Your precepts."** (Ps. 119:44-45)

Seeking freedom to live a 'lawless' life is like a fish seeking to live outside of water. We will soon find ourselves gasping for breath.

CHAPTER THREE

BIRTH OF A KINGDOM OF PRIESTS (COHANIM)

Passover was the birth of Israel as a "kingdom of priests and a holy nation." (Exodus 19:6)

Jacob *(Yaacov)* led a small band of seventy souls into Egypt, but they marched out a nation of several million. Over 600,000 adult males marched forth with a high hand out of their bondage in Egypt. The blood of the Passover lamb redeemed and saved the Israelites in order that they could freely serve the Lord their God. This was the whole purpose of their redemption – freedom to serve the living God, rather than the Pharaoh. The Lord commanded through Moses and Aaron,

> **"Let My people go that they may serve me."**
> (Ex. 8:20)

She was still in her infancy when Israel came out of Egypt, but the stage of delivery was complete. Now she needed to grow and mature under the care and guidance of her heavenly Abba (father).

Those in Messiah, saved by His blood, the Lamb who was slain, are also called a:

> **"...chosen generation, a royal priesthood, a holy nation, His own special people, that you may proclaim the praises of Him who called you out of darkness into His marvelous light..."** (1 Pet. 2:9)

All are saved by the grace of God, through His mercy; but so too do we all need to learn, under the guidance of the Holy Spirit, how to live a holy life, pleasing unto God. How are we to do this? There is only one answer – grace! Only by His grace can we even breathe our next breath, let alone walk in obedience and holiness. This grace has been provided through a New Covenant, promised long ago through the Hebrew prophets. But what was wrong with the 'Old Covenant'? Nothing was wrong with the covenant itself; it was simply Israel's inability to keep it that was at fault.

Mount Sinai

Israel came out of Egypt and set their sights on the Promised Land, but יהוה (*YHVH*) had a pit stop in mind first – Mount Sinai. It was here that Israel entered into a holy covenant with her God. Instead of a protective, fatherly provider, Elohim became the ravishing bridegroom. Israel stood under the chuppah (wedding canopy) covering of the cloud and was asked, *"Do you take this God to be your God and do you promise to obey His word?"* And Israel answered, *"We do!"* (Ex. 24:3) But it was shortly after this pledge of fidelity that Israel was already committing adultery with a foreign god, the golden calf. If not for the desperate intercession of Moses, God would have destroyed this fledgling nation entirely. Time after time after time, Israel as a nation broke her word and walked in disobedience. The trip from Egypt to the Promised Land, which should have taken eleven days, took instead forty years of wandering in the wilderness. They wandered and suffered and then they died. This is the 'not so celebrated' aspect of

Passover, but it bears studying since it may serve as an important warning to us.

Bodies in the Wilderness

Passover is generally celebrated as a joyous festival, of liberation, freedom, and deliverance. And it is. But there exists another side to Passover that we must also keep in mind. After the heady exhilaration of sudden freedom came the soul-sucking journey through the wilderness. The fate of those delivered from slavery in Egypt is not something we like to consider. The tragedy is that even though they all came out of Egypt and traveled under the cloud; all passed through the sea of Reeds and all ate the manna and drank the water that the Lord provided in the desert, only two courageous souls made it into the Promised Land. The rest perished in the wilderness.

> **"Moreover brethren, I do not want you to be unaware that all our fathers were under the cloud, all passed through the sea, all were baptized into Moses in the cloud and in the sea, all ate the same spiritual food, and all drank the same spiritual drink. For they drank of that spiritual Rock that followed them, and that Rock was Messiah. But with most of them God was not well pleased, for their bodies were scattered in the wilderness."**
> (1 Cor. 10:1-5)

Why? The answer is simple – disobedience! These unfortunate Israelites should stand as examples to us:

> **"Now these things became our examples, to the intent that we should not lust after evil things as**

they also lusted. And do not become idolaters, as were some of them… Nor let us commit sexual immorality, as some of them did… nor let us tempt Messiah, as some of them also tempted and were destroyed by serpents; nor complain, as some of them also complained, and were destroyed by the destroyer. Now all these things happened to them as examples, and they were written for our admonition, upon whom the ends of the ages have come."** (1 Corinthians 10:6 -11)

Complaint Department

Complained? They were destroyed because they complained? Oye! Complaining seems to be a well entrenched behavior pattern, not only in Jewish people, but also within the entire human race. Can complaining actually provoke God's wrath? The Word of God testifies that it certainly can and does. As the children of Israel journeyed around the land of Adom[1], their souls became very discouraged along the way. (Numbers 21:4) And so they began to complain:

> **"Why have you brought us up out of Egypt to die in the wilderness? For there is no food and no water, and our soul loathes this worthless bread."**
> (Num. 21:5)

It is very easy to sit back in judgment on the Israelites, clucking our tongues in indignation at the immature and ungrateful

---

[1] 'Adom' (meaning red) is the Hebrew 'nickname' for Esau. It became the term used for the descendants of Esau - many of whom constitute the Arabic people of today. Usually written as Edom in most English Bibles.

manner in which they reacted. But I challenge anyone to actually put on your hikers and walk with me along the dry, hard, crusty, mountainous Israeli wilderness without feeling somewhat forlorn and frightened in your soul. We took the family camping one Chanukah to Eilat and set up our tent near a mountain. Each morning, my son would wake up with the dawn and go exploring with the other boys. But one day, he asked me to go with him. He showed me their 'fort' and all the scraps of junk they had managed to burn with a packet of matches. Then he asked me to walk a little further with him over to another 'neat place'. I began the journey, but looking upon the vast expanse of barrenness, I lost heart and gave up. So too, do we lose heart and want to give up (if we could) in the midst of trials and difficulties that we must walk through. We cannot see an end in sight; the way is too dry, too lonely, and too barren. And so we begin to complain. And this is not pleasing to God when we voice our doubt and unbelief rather than our trust in Him. It wasn't actually true that the Israelites had no food or water; God had provided for His children but they were not satisfied. So too do we murmur in dissatisfaction with what God has provided, despising the same old lousy manna, instead of gratefully receiving His faithful provision and trusting Him to provide more or 'different' in His perfect way and timing.

Beware of Discouragement

Idolatry, lust, and sexual immorality – these are fairly obvious sins that most of us can deal with in our lives as Believers. But do we consider that complaining, murmuring, and ingratitude are equally grievous sins to God?

> **"So the Lord sent fiery serpents among the people, and they bit the people; and many of the people of Israel died."** (Num. 21:6)

We must beware of the danger of discouragement, lest it cause us to sin. What, then, do we do when we become discouraged? We remember Yeshua on the cross:

> **"For consider Him who endured such hostility from sinners against Himself, lest you become weary and discouraged in your souls."** (Heb. 12:3)

The Cure

What brought healing to the people of Israel from the venom of the serpents? The Lord told Moses to make a snake and put it upon a pole; anyone who is bitten can look at it and live.

> **"So Moses made a bronze snake and put it up on a pole. Then when anyone was bitten by a snake and looked at the bronze snake, he lived."** (Num. 21:9)

When Adam and Chava (Eve) gave in to the serpent in the Garden of Eden, they infected the blood of the human race with the snake's evil venom. We are all contaminated with sin for which there is only one cure – we must look up to Him who hung on a cross to cleanse us from our sins. All who do this will live.

> **"And as Moses lifted up the serpent in the wilderness, even so must the Son of Man be lifted up, that whoever believes in Him should not perish but have eternal life."** (John 3:14-15)

You see, the real issue at stake here is not our physical salvation, whether we live or die on this earth, for we are only temporary residents here. We walk this earth as strangers and aliens in temporal bodies, but our real destiny is eternity. Our true home is with our God in the New Jerusalem– a place where there no longer exists sorrow or pain, sickness or death; where His hand will wipe away every tear from every eye.

> **"God Himself will be with them and be their God. And God will wipe away every tear from their eyes; there shall be no more death, nor sorrow, nor crying. There shall be no more pain, for the former things have passed away."** (Rev. 21:3-4)

Because of His great love for humanity, God sent His only son, Yeshua, to die that we might live eternally with Him.

> **"For God so loved the world that He gave His only begotten son, that whoever believes in Him should not perish but have everlasting life."** (John 3:16)

And so we celebrate Passover as a great festival of liberation, both physical and spiritual, but we also must keep in mind the example of the Israelites' fate after their salvation. Too many people have been saved by the blood of the Lamb, delivered from Egypt, baptized through the sea and headed towards the Promised Land but along the way they are dying. Their bodies are scattered all over the wilderness because of their sins. God does not wish for any to perish but to repent and have life.

I don't believe this means that we would actually lose our salvation and go to hell because of a little griping. God didn't send the Israelites back into Egypt to serve Pharoah again. But they did finish the course of their lives without ever entering the Promised Land. When we murmur and complain in doubt, unbelief and ungratefulness, God cannot bring us into the promised place of all the blessings He has for us. It is not He who is withholding the blessings or not making good on His promises. It is us who refuse to align ourselves with the divine flow of faith and trust in a good heavenly Father, who keep ourselves from inheriting the promises of God for our lives. If we want to see all the wondrous blessings God has for us, to fulfill His plan for our lives, to live out our divine purpose and destiny, to enjoy our inheritance, then we need to enter His rest through believing in His power and trusting in His mercy.

Salvation Not Enough

I hesitate to even write these words, lest a lynch mob find me and finish me off! But the truth is that our salvation through the blood of the Lamb, by the grace and mercy of God, (just as it was for the Israelites) is only the first step along our journey. It is the starting point; the pushing of the eject button. We are flung out of Egypt, but we still need to make it into the Promised Land and it is sometimes a tortuous journey. It is not enough to be saved; God's will is that we would come to a knowledge of the truth. (1 Tim. 2:4)

May we celebrate Passover in joy knowing that this is a step of faith and obedience, in coming closer to the Truth. Thus we who are in Yeshua regard the Passover as not only a physical deliverance, but also a spiritual liberation to serve our God as He has commanded us, and not according to the dictates of man.

CHAPTER FOUR

COVENANT

Now that we know for a certainty that the Bible commands the celebration of the Passover, a pressing issue which needs to be settled is, "*Who should keep it*? To who is the command of the Lord directed? Who are the ones the apostle Paul is exhorting to keep the Feast?" (1 Cor. 5:8) Is the command strictly for the Jewish people or is does it apply also to non-Jewish followers of Yeshua? If the Passover is just a quaint, Jewish tradition, then we will approach our study as simply an interesting intellectual exercise in theology or comparative religion. However, we will perceive the information in an entirely different manner if the Passover is seen as personally relevant to us. In fact, it may become a life-changing experience, as many have found out! Is the Passover just a "Jewish version of Easter?" Is the Passover and are the other feasts exclusively for the Jewish people or 'Jewish wanna-be's'? To determine answers to these questions, we need to return to the beginning of the Bible to examine the issue of covenant.

In the beginning (*B'reisheet*), God made an everlasting covenant with our forefather Abram. Let us not forget that Abraham, Isaac and Jacob, were not technically Jewish! To be Jewish meant to descend from the tribe of Judah (*Yehudah*) and this son of Yaacov (Jacob) had not even been born yet! God called Abram out of Ur of the Chaldees. The nation of Israel did not yet exist. Only once Yaacov (Jacob)'s name was changed to Yisrael (Israel) after wrestling all night with an angel, did even the word 'Yisrael' (Israel) come into being. And it was through Jacob, the designated heir rather than Esau,[1] that the divine covenant then passed to his twelve sons –the fathers of the twelve tribes of Israel. Abram entered into divine covenant with the Creator, thereby inheriting the blessings of this covenant. This was a blood covenant, as the animals were cut in two and יהוה (*YHVH)* Himself, in the form of a smoking firepot,[2] passed through the pieces – an ancient way of sealing a covenant. Abram was fast asleep while God performed this holy ceremony, demonstrating that the promises depended exclusively upon the faithfulness of the Almighty not on the behavior of Abram or his seed. God granted Abraham wonderful promises; he would be the father of a great nation (goy gadol) (Gen. 12:2). Actually, the word 'goy' can mean nation or Gentile. He promised Abraham that, although he appeared childless even in old age, his descendants would be as numerous as the dust of the earth, and the stars in the sky (Gen. 15:5). Abram believed the Lord and it was counted unto him as righteousness. Obviously, this promise is not fulfilled only in the small minority of the Jewish population. Abraham was given the promise of becoming a father of many nations. The Hebrew words used here are 'Av hamon goyim'. Av means father; hamon is more than many – it means multitudes! And goyim, as mentioned, could mean Gentiles or nations. The promises and blessings of Abraham are not exclusively for the Jewish people but for all who will enter into covenant with God through the Jewish Messiah.

> **"…that the blessing of Abraham might come upon the Gentiles in Messiah Yeshua…"** (Gal. 3:14)

---

1 Gen. 29:13
2 Gen. 15:17

Some Believers are experiencing a real identity crisis in these days. Who are we? Are we grafted in Gentiles? Are we part of the lost tribes of Israel (Ephraim)? The truth is, that if we are in the Messiah, then it makes no difference whether we are Jew or Gentile – we are:

> "Abraham's seed and heirs according to the promise." (Gal. 3:29)

Covenant of Promise Not Annulled By the Law

Some would believe that this covenant of promise has been cancelled by the sinfulness of the nation of Israel, or worse yet, because the Jews rejected Jesus! According to the covenant made at Sinai through Moses (The Mosaic Covenant), the Israelites willingly entered into a conditional covenant of blessings for obedience and curses for disobedience. We know from Biblical history that the nation of Israel certainly did not live up to their end of the agreement. They fell into idolatry and profaned the Sabbath. For this disobedience, God was forced to carry out the punishment of exile and bondage. God foretold the bondage that Abram's descendants would endure in Egypt:

> "Know certainly that your descendants will be strangers in a land that is not theirs, and will serve them, and they will afflict them four hundred years. And also the nation whom they serve I will judge; afterward they shall come out with great possessions." (Gen. 15:13-14)

Isn't it ironic, that even though God uses nations as instruments of His divine punishment upon Israel, He still judges these nations afterwards for touching the 'apple of His eye'. God will judge every nation that has mistreated His people. These four hundred years of bondage, however, could not annul God's covenant with Abram; these promises are absolutely unconditional.

> **"The Law (Torah), which was four hundred and thirty years later, cannot annul the covenant that was confirmed before by God in Messiah, that it should make the promise of no effect...but God gave it to Abraham by promise."** (Gal. 3:17-18)

God does not break His promises, and we are children of promise! Although the Torah carries within it a covenant of blessings for obedience and curses for disobedience, God's covenant of blessing with Abraham and His descendants still holds fast. He will make good on His promises to all His people IN HIS TIME.

> **"For thus says the Lord: 'Just as I have brought all this great calamity on this people, so I will bring on them all the good that I have promised them.'"** (Jer. 32:42)

Yes, Gentiles in Messiah Yeshua have joined the Jewish people in becoming the seed of Abraham, but God's covenant with Israel also holds. If one runs into someone of the persuasion who believes Israel to be rejected forever by God for their rejection of Jesus as Messiah, all one needs to do is take them outside and ask them to look up. If they still see a sun in the sky by day or a moon and stars in the sky by night, then they may be assured that God has not cast off the descendants of Jacob and David (Israel).

> Thus says the Lord: 'If My covenant is not with day and night, and if I have not appointed the ordinances of heaven and earth, then I will cast

> **away the descendants of Jacob and David My servant…For I will cause their captives to return and will have mercy on them.'"** (Jer. 33:23-26)

One day - in God's timing and not our own, He will send back the Messiah and bring back the captives of the descendants of Jacob (Israel). This, of course, brings up the issue, Who is Israel? The apostle Paul said that not all who claim to be of Israel are truly Israel.

> **"For they are not all Israel who are of Israel, nor are they all children because they are the seed of Abraham; but "In Isaac your seed shall be called." That is, those who are the children of the flesh, these are not the children of God but the children of the promise are counted as the seed."** (Romans 9:6-8)

In God's Kingdom, it is not the flesh or physical lineage that counts, but our openness to being Fathered by God, becoming His children by promise.

CHAPTER FIVE

THE PROPHETIC MEANING OF PASSOVER

The Lion of Judah Defends Jerusalem

The Word of God promises a more glorious Passover one day than even that of the coming out of Egypt. This will be the day that the Lord Himself will defend Jerusalem and will pass-over her!

> "As a lion roars, and a young lion over his prey... so the Lord of hosts will come down to fight for Mount Zion and for its hill. Like birds flying about, so will the Lord of hosts (YHVH Tz'va'ot) defend Jerusalem. Defending, He will also deliver it. Passing over (pasach) {פסח}, He will preserve it." (Isaiah 31:4-5)

This is the meaning of the Hebrew word Pesach, the name of the Feast of Passover – to pass, spring, or jump over. All over Jerusalem during the week before Passover 2002, life-sized, colorful statues of lions appeared. Their message is clear – the Lion of Judah (symbol of Jerusalem and one of the representations of the God of Israel) will one day come to defend Israel from her enemies when the Messiah returns. Then the Lord will bring

His people back to the Land and not leave even one behind. (Ezek. 39:28). The manner in which the Lord will accomplish this amazing feat of bringing all His people out of exile is once again - with fury poured out!

Fury Poured Out Again

> "As I live, says the Lord God, 'surely with a mighty hand, with an outstretched arm, and with fury poured out, I will rule over you. I will bring you out from the peoples and gather you out of the countries where you are scattered, with a mighty hand and with an outstretched arm, and with fury poured out.'" (Ezek. 20:33-34)

Do you hear the Passover terminology used in these passages? ...a mighty hand...an outstretched arm...fury poured out.... They are the same words used to describe the deliverance of the Israelites from Egypt. Freedom is not without a price. Yeshua tells us to count the cost. But one day, remaining in exile will no longer be an option for the people of יהוה (YHVH). He will pour out His fury and defeat all the gods of Egypt in order to bring His people out of captivity.

Long ago, God heard the groaning of the children of Israel in their bondage and had compassion on them and remembered His COVENANT with them and rescued them:

> "I am the Lord יהוה (YHVH); I will bring you out from under the burdens of the Egyptians, I will rescue you from their bondage, and I will redeem you with an outstretched arm and with great judgments...And I will bring you into the land which I swore to give to

> Abraham, Isaac, and Jacob; and I will give it to you as a heritage; I am יהוה **(YHVH)."** (Ex. 6:6, 8)

A Greater Passover

As glorious and awesome as was this great Passover, the prophetic Word of God promises an even greater Passover. The days are coming that we will no longer refer to God as the One who brought us out of Egypt, but as the One who brought us out of all the countries of our exile to dwell in our own land.

> **"Therefore, behold, the days are coming, says the Lord, that they shall no longer say, 'As the Lord lives who brought up the children of Israel from the land of Egypt', but, 'As the Lord lives who brought up and led the descendants of the house of Israel from the north country and from all the countries where I had driven them.' And they shall dwell in their own land."** (Jer. 23:7-8)

IN THESE DAYS (the coming of the Messiah) Judah (the house of Yehudah - the Jews of today) will be saved and Israel will finally dwell safely, no longer harassed by the painful thorns and briers of Islamic terror. (Jer. 23:6) When will this day come? It will come when the 'Branch' (*Tzemach*) of righteousness is raised up to sit on the throne of David. This eternal heir of David's throne was born as a son upon the earth long ago to a Jewish maiden named Miryam. (Is. 7:14) He will carry the mantle of the government of the entire earth upon his shoulders and will rule on David's throne forever in the Messianic Kingdom. (Is. 9:6-7)

This Messiah will execute judgment and righteousness in the earth. His name is YHVH Tz'dkeinu, which means the Lord our Righteousness. We know this to be Yeshua, for He is a cohen (priest) after the order of Malchi-Tzedek (which means My King of Righteousness). (Jer. 23:5-6)

> **"You are a cohen (priest) forever according to the order of Malchi-Tzedek."** (Ps. 110:4)

This priest-king of righteousness will execute ungodly leaders and rulers in the day of His wrath as He judges among the nations. Yeshua was raised up according to this order of Malchi-Tzedek, and not according to the order of Aaron, the Levitical priesthood. He has come, not according to the law of a fleshly commandment, but according to the power of eternal life! (Heb. 7:11-16)

The days are coming, and perhaps sooner than we are prepared for, when the wrath of the Lamb will fall upon the earth and He will execute judgment.

> **"Fall on us and hide us from the face of Him who sits on the throne and from the wrath of the Lamb! For the great day of His wrath has come, and who is able to stand?"** (Rev. 6:16-17)

All those not covered by the blood of the Passover Lamb will be subject to the plagues that will one day be poured out again upon the earth. (Rev. 8:7-Rev. 11)

At this time, God will use the plagues to execute judgment again on the gods of this earth to bring His people out of exile and into the Promised Land. The children of Israel will once again face the wilderness testing with the Lord.

> **"'And I will bring you into the wilderness of the peoples, and there I will plead My case with you face to face. Just as I pleaded My case with your fathers in**

> the wilderness of the land of Egypt, so I will plead
> My case with you,' says the Lord God."
> (Ezek. 20:35-36)

Will all make it? Unfortunately not. A terrible purging will take place of those who refuse to come under the bond of the New Covenant sealed in the blood of the Lamb, Yeshua.

> "I will make you pass under the rod, and I will bring you into the bond of the covenant; I will purge the rebels from among you, and those who transgress against Me; I will bring them out of the country where they dwell, but they shall not enter the land of Israel. Then you will know that I am YHVH (יהוה)." (Ezek. 20:37-38)

One day we will all feast at the marriage supper of the Lamb. This will be the most wonderful and greatest Passover Seder of all times! **"Let us be glad and rejoice and give Him glory, for the marriage of the Lamb has come, and His wife has made herself ready. Blessed are those who are called to the marriage supper of the Lamb..."** (Rev. 19:7, 9)

CHAPTER SIX

LET ALL YOUR MALES BE CIRCUMCISED...

There is still one thorny issue standing in the way of us achieving unity in celebrating the Passover. I almost hate to mention it, but there it is in scriptures, that is, the issue of circumcision.

> **"And when a stranger dwells with you and wants to keep the Passover to the Lord, let all his males be circumcised, and then let him come near and keep it; and he shall be as a native of the land. For no uncircumcised person shall eat it."** (Ex. 12:48)

Now before you go out and make an appointment for your circumcision, let's study this issue. Circumcision surfaced as a point of great contention in the early community of 'The Way' (evidenced by the need for the Jerusalem council described in Acts 15). Some of the Jewish Believers insisted that those coming to faith through Yeshua must first be circumcised in order to be accepted into the fold. Others held to the other major Jewish school of thought of the day that the most important requirement for conversion to Judaism is that of the Mikvah (ritual water immersion). We must keep in mind that at this point, a religion called 'Christianity' did not exist. Followers of Yeshua (The Way) were simply another sect of Judaism and those who wanted to join them were considered converts. Even today, the conversion issue rages on. Who can become part of Israel and how is such a process carried out? The Orthodox Jewish sect in Israel does not recognize the conversions of other sects such as Conservative and Reform Judaism (and certainly not Messianic Judaism!). In March 2002, the High Courts of Israel ruled that these conversions are legitimate and the State of Israel will recognize Gentiles who go through Conservative or Reform conversion programs as officially Jewish. This has brought a furor from the Orthodox Jewish leaders who then refuse to authorize Israeli identity cards if they list the nationality of Conservative or Reform converts as 'Jewish'. You are perhaps receiving a glimpse of the argumentative nature of the Jewish people. I just found out that the same Hebrew word 'Midrash' is used for commentary on the Bible and 'playground'. Indeed, arguing, especially about Biblical or religious issues is almost a game to some Jewish people. And one can see by visiting Israel and observing the people on the streets, in their shops, and especially in their cars, that arguing is a 'national sport'. A popular expression says that if there are two Jews in a room, there will likely be at least three opinions. How the Jerusalem Council ever came to a consensus is beyond me!

And so we can see that they were probably struggling in the early congregations, just as they continue to do now, with the issue of conversion. It is easy to see why some considered circumcision an essential requirement of following the God of Israel. The Bible takes a strong stand here; any male children not circumcised in the flesh are considered cut off from the nation of Israel for having broken the covenant. The command to circumcise is eternal and forever for the descendants of Abraham.

> **"This is My covenant which you shall keep, between Me and you and your descendants after you: Every male child among you shall be circumcised; and you shall be circumcised in the flesh of your foreskins,**

> and it shall be a sign of the covenant between Me
> and you. He who is eight days old among you shall
> be circumcised...And the uncircumcised male child,
> who is not circumcised in the flesh of his foreskin,
> that person shall be cut off from his people; he has
> broken My covenant." (Gen. 17:10-14)

A Bridegroom of Blood

How seriously did God really take this command? Well, if we look at the example of Moses, our deliverer in the Passover story, God tried to kill him because he had not obeyed the commandment to circumcise his son, Gershum. (Ex. 4:24-26) 'Ger' is the Hebrew word for 'stranger' and 'shum' means 'there'. Moses called his son Ger-shum because he was a stranger there. And yet it was so important for Moses to walk in obedience to the sign of the covenant before going as a deliverer to the nation of Israel that God sought to kill him! Amazing, isn't it! Why didn't Moses circumcise his son? It was because of the reluctance of his Gentile wife, Zipporah. Seeing that Moses would die, she finally gave in and cut off her son's foreskin with a sharp stone and struck his legs with the bloody foreskin and said, *"You are a bridegroom of blood to me!"* If we see Moses as representing the Jewish side of the 'One new man' and Zipporah as the 'Gentile' side, we can see the potential for contention over the issue of circumcision. The keeping of the 'law' or Torah is a contentious issue for some; and yet we are warned not to get into foolish (stupid) controversies over the Torah:

> "But avoid disputes, genealogies, contentions,
> and strivings about the law (Torah), for they are
> unprofitable and useless." (Titus 3:9)

Spirit Not Letter

Of what value is the circumcision? It is profitable if one keeps the Torah, but if one is a lawless person (breaks the Torah), then his circumcision counts for nothing. On the contrary, an uncircumcised person who keeps the Torah is counted as if circumcised, since he proves the law is written on his heart according to the New Covenant.

> **"For circumcision is indeed profitable if you keep the law; but if you are a breaker of the law, your circumcision has become uncircumcision. Therefore, if an uncircumcised man keeps the requirements of the law, will not his uncircumcision be counted as circumcision?"** (Rom. 2:25-26)

The apostle Paul goes so far as to declare a Jew as not one outwardly circumcised in the flesh, but one who is inwardly circumcised in their heart,

> **"...in the Spirit, not in the letter; whose praise is not from men but from God."** (Rom. 2:29)

Paul also tells us that there is only one God who will justify the circumcised by faith and the uncircumcised also through faith. (Rom. 3:30). Does this faith nullify the Torah? Paul says,

> **"Certainly not! On the contrary, we establish the Torah."** (Rom. 3:31)

In true Jewish fashion, Paul asks and answers his own question,

> "Does this blessedness (of the man to whom God imputes righteousness apart from works) then come upon the circumcised only, or upon the uncircumcised also?" (Rom. 4:9)

He then goes on to remind us that Abraham's faith was accounted to him as righteousness while still in an uncircumcised state. The sign of the circumcision then acted as the seal of the righteousness of his faith which he had while still uncircumcised.

The Final Verdict

What then is the final verdict of the apostles? Obviously, the school of thought favoring the mikvah as the essential requirement of salvation rather than circumcision won out.

> "He who believes <u>and is baptized</u> (immersed in the waters of the mikvah) will be saved." (Mark 16:16)

Even Yeshua said unless one is born <u>of water and the spirit</u>, he cannot enter the Kingdom (John 3:5). This would seem to indicate that the ritual water immersion of the mikvah, or baptism, is necessary for entrance into the Kingdom, not circumcision. And yet Ezekiel gives a word from the Lord indicating that circumcision may continue to be an issue even at the time of the Millennial Temple:

> "No foreigner, uncircumcised in heart <u>or uncircumcised in flesh</u>, shall enter My sanctuary, <u>including any foreigner</u> who is among the children of Israel." (Ezek. 44:9)

It must be made very clear, however, that circumcision is not a salvation issue!

Yeshua's Circumcision

If circumcision is not required for us to enter heaven, is it then a valid practice for Believers? If we look at the example of Yeshua, we may see that his parents obeyed the command to have him circumcised on the eighth day of his life. Traditionally, a Jewish male child is not given his name until the time of his brit millah (bris), which translates literally from the Hebrew as 'covenant of the Word'. We did not officially 'let the cat out of the bag' about what name we had chosen for our newborn son, Avi-ad, until his brit millah on the eighth day. At the time of Yeshua's circumcision, he was also given His name.

> **"And when eight days were completed for the circumcision of the Child, His name was called Yeshua, the name given by the angels before He was conceived in the womb."** (Luke 2:21)

Keeping the Commandments is What Matters

What about those called into the Kingdom while uncircumcised? Should they have the circumcision performed? The letters of Paul discourage such a practice:

> **"Was anyone called while circumcised? Let him not become uncircumcised. Was anyone called while uncircumcised? Let him not be circumcised. Circumcision is nothing and uncircumcision is nothing, but keeping the commandments of God is what matters."** (1 Cor. 7:18-19)

What Paul is saying here, is that circumcision is not the point; what is more important is obedience to the Torah! This is obviously an extremely delicate matter, and not simply because of the point of anatomy that we're dealing with! I know of one Believer who, under pressure from an Orthodox Jewish group that he studied with, went through with his circumcision as an adult. He eventually ended up denying Yeshua (in Hebrew means salvation) and falling away from the faith. Then again, Timothy voluntarily had himself circumcised in order to more effectively act as a witness to the Jewish people, and he remained a faithful servant of the Lord! And so there are no black and white answers.

Circumcision of the Heart

If we may return full circle to the issue of Passover and circumcision, I believe that taking a doctrinally hard line, black and white stance on this issue only leads to divisiveness and self-righteous, religious pride. I know of one ministry that states as a written requirement that any who want to partake of the Passover with them must first be circumcised. Now, besides the fact that we wonder how they are going to enforce such a requirement (what will they do – check at the door?) such a rigid practice sticks to the letter and misses the spirit.

> **"In Him you were also circumcised with the circumcision made without hands, by putting off the body of the sins of the flesh, by the circumcision of Messiah, buried with Him in baptism..."**
> (Col. 2:11-12)

And so it is true – one cannot partake of the Passover while uncircumcised. But if any man has been saved through the blood of Yeshua, buried with Him in baptism, and raised to new life in the Messiah, then I believe he may answer in all good conscience, *"Yes, I am circumcised in the Messiah and fully eligible to partake of the Passover as an equal heir of those circumcised in the flesh. The Torah of God is in my heart and my desire is to keep the commandment of God."*

Shalom and welcome to the celebration of Passover - God's appointed time.

CHAPTER SEVEN

PASSOVER: A SEASON FOR HARVEST

One of the most wonderful things to discover about the Feasts (Moadim) of the Lord יהוה (YHVH) is that the Spirit of God still moves along the same theme as the Feast, even when people don't realize it! I remember being a new Believer, and attending a Bible College in a large, evangelical, charismatic church. I was hungry to learn as much about this faith in Yeshua as I could. An anointed Bible teacher, who yielded the word of God like a two-edged sword to cut all the sin and uncleanness out of our lives, taught the course. She began to preach about the one day a year that the Old Testament High priest (Cohen haGadol) could enter the Holy of Holies. She claimed this to be such a holy place that they would tie bells on the cohen's tunic and a rope around his ankle so that they could drag him out in case he dropped dead through some religious indiscretion. I became so excited; I raised my hand and began bouncing in my seat, *"Ooh, ooh, teacher, teacher!"* I burned with the zeal to share that this very day on the Hebrew calendar happened to be the Day of Atonement (Yom Kippur) of which she spoke. Needless to say, my comments were met with less enthusiasm, as the supervisor of the Bible College happened to be the son of a man imprisoned for spreading his racist, anti-Semitic teachings among his high school student classes! God has a real sense of humor placing this Jewish girl in this particular church to be discipled.

The Master Craftsman

I have noted this interesting phenomenon so often; I have become convinced that the Spirit of God still works according to His specifically appointed moadim (times). This is one reason why it is so important to respect the Creator as a divine craftsman who has set His feasts as precious gems in the circular watch-piece of the cycle of time. We move these around and change them only to our own peril or loss.

The Spirit of God is at work during Passover in this day, as He was 3500 years ago in Egypt. On that First Passover He worked His salvation through the blood of the Lamb that was slain, to save multitudes from the coming wrath of God.

Just as some nominal Christians celebrate Christmas and know about Jesus, but have not entered into a personal relationship with Him, nor fully understand what He did for us, so do many nominal Jewish people (if we can call them that) celebrate Passover without understanding the spiritual principles behind salvation through the blood of the Lamb. Passover is the perfect time to explain this truth: The blood of the lambs saved the Israelite families from certain death. It was not their good deeds that saved them, but only the sign of the blood.

> **"Now the blood shall be a sign for you on the houses where you are. And when I see the blood, I will pass over you; and the plague shall not be on you to destroy you when I strike the land of Egypt."**
> (Ex. 12:13)

Seder meals are held all over the world to fulfill the commandment to remember, proclaim, and celebrate our glorious salvation, deliverance, and rescue from Egypt. But often the centrality of the lamb and its blood for salvation is ironically ignored or "passed-over."

Without understanding the role of the Passover Lamb, the primary meaning of the Passover is lost amidst all the ceremony, rituals, food and wine. Only when the blinders are removed and we see the Messiah in the Passover does the Seder take on its rich and beautiful significance. This is what happened to one Jewish woman who came to see her Messiah in the Passover and seek refuge in the covering of the blood of the Lamb.

The Seeker

Calling herself only 'The Seeker', she began corresponding with me under the cover of anonymity afforded by e-mail after finding one of my books in a Christian bookstore. She asked me about my testimony, my faith in Yeshua, and how this harmonizes with my Jewish heritage. We discussed family reactions, theological doctrines and other issues, but she seemed to never come to the point of decision - until she read a Messianic commentary on the account of the Passover. It was at this point that the blinders fell away and the Seeker found what she was seeking all along. She has been growing in the Lord ever since, and although she still struggles with family issues over her faith she stands firm in Yeshua.

CHAPTER EIGHT

THE FEASTS OF יהוה[1]

"Well," some may say, "that is wonderful that some Jewish people are able to find the Messiah in Passover, but how is the feast relevant for a Christian who already 'knows Jesus'?" This is a good question. Passover (or Pesach in Hebrew) has long been considered a Jewish festival or time of celebration. When the students in public schools are taking their Easter break from school, usually the Jewish ones would take off at the same time, but to celebrate Passover instead. Is it really God's intention, however, to have His covenant people celebrating in different ways and on different days? The New Testament says that His desire is to make 'one new man' out of the two covenant people groups – Jews and Christians.

> **"So as to create in Himself one new man from the two, thus making peace…"** (Eph. 2:15)

---

[1] This is the Hebrew name of the One whom we usually call God. His real name (YHVH in English without vowels) is usually translated 'LORD' in most Bibles.

One Law (Torah) and One Custom

How will this be accomplished? Will the one new man, neither Jew nor Gentile, be created through the abolishment of God's laws and commandments? This contradicts the words of Yeshua who told us that He never came to abolish the law (Torah) but to fulfill it and that whoever teaches anyone to break even the least of the commandments will be the least in the Kingdom (Matt. 5:17-19). I don't know about you, but I don't want to occupy the least position in the Kingdom so I am not going to teach you that the commandments of יהוה YHVH are abolished in Yeshua! The only true way of reconciling these two groups is to return to a Biblical model of worship; and the only way to accomplish this is through obedience to His word with the help of the Holy Spirit. Even in the Old Testament, all people were welcome to join in the ways of Israel in worshipping their Elohim, but there could be only one law and one standard.

> **"One ordinance shall be for you of the assembly and for the stranger who dwells with you, an ordinance forever throughout your generations; as you are, so shall the stranger be before the Lord. One law and one custom shall be for you and for the stranger who dwells with you."** (Num. 15:15-16)

The book of Ephesians describes how Gentiles without the Messiah are aliens from the commonwealth of Israel and strangers from the covenants of promise, having no hope and without Elohim in the world (what a terrible state to be in!).

> **"But now in Messiah Yeshua you who once were far off** (from the commonwealth of Israel, the covenants of promise, and Elohim) **have been brought near by the blood of Messiah."** (Eph. 2:11-13)

Isn't it wonderful that all strangers may become part of Israel through the blood of Israel's Messiah? But now there must only be one ordinance, one law (torah) and one custom. This includes celebrating the Feasts of the Lord.

The truth is that these are not exclusively 'Jewish' feasts and festivals, but they are the Lord's. He states clearly, *"these are My moadim (appointed times)."* (Lev. 23:2) These do not belong to a specific people group any more than the Bible or the Messiah is limited to the Jewish people. (Some might like to consider these their private property, but in actual fact they belong to the Lord, and He accepts all people groups without favoritism through the Messiah). And so celebrating the Feasts of the Lord, including Passover, is a Biblically correct thing to do, no matter what the local church says!

Let the Little Children Come Unto Me

It was such a wonderful experience to hold a Passover Seder in a Church for the nursery and children's group. There is little more precious in this world than the wonderment of children. We had great fun searching for the chametz (pieces of bread) hidden in the room, giving out prizes, singing 'Go down Moses' and 'Let my people go!". But when we came to the songs like 'I've been redeemed by the blood of the lamb', or 'Lamb of God', the children were puzzled. Why do they call Jesus a lamb? No one knew. Only once we explained how the innocent Passover lambs were slain and the blood placed on the doorposts of the Israelite homes did they begin to connect Yeshua's death on the cross as the innocent 'Lamb of God.' It was beautiful to see their faces light up in recognition and understanding. But in a way, I felt sad that all these children were being cheated from their heritage and a fuller understanding of Yeshua by the tragedy of the divorce between Judaism and Christianity. Once again, as in any divorce, the children are the ones suffering the most. We owe it to our children to explain and celebrate the Passover with them, in the context of our Jewish roots in the Jewish Messiah, so that they may more fully understand what He has done in saving us from the wrath of God.

The Lamb of God

Keeping the Passover is not simply a memorial celebration of the Israelites' rescue from slavery in Egypt; it also stands as a bold proclamation of the Messiah as the Passover Lamb. When John (Yochanan) saw Yeshua coming towards him at the Jordan where John was immersing people in water, he said,

> **"Behold! The Lamb of God who takes away the sin of the world!"** (John 1:29)

Generational Evangelism

One of the expressly stated reasons for celebrating the Passover is for the purpose of teaching our children Biblical truths.

> **"And it shall be, when your children say to you, 'What do you mean by this service?' That you shall say, 'It is the Passover sacrifice of the Lord, who passed over the houses of the children of Israel in Egypt when He struck the Egyptians and delivered our households.'"** (Ex. 12:26)

Children are naturally inquisitive and who knows this better than the One who created and fashioned them in the womb? As a former teacher, I learned that children learn best, and we hold their interest longer when a lesson is 'hands on'; that is, when they can feel, taste, smell, and touch their subject. The Passover service is, therefore, a perfect learning tool for children. The one thing children don't like to be is bored! (Who does?) They have little tolerance for sitting still and being 'preached at'. But to drink the wine, taste the food, dip the greens, choke on the horseradish, watch everyone else choke on the horseradish, sing the songs, run around looking for bits of bread, hold the lamb shank bone in their hands – this is what holds the interest of children and teaches them the true meaning of Passover. I encourage you to hold a Passover service as commanded, to answer the questions of our children when they look at us a little strange and ask, *"Why are you guys doing all these weird and wonderful things on this night?"* (mah nishtana paraphrase)[2] Hopefully we will then have answers that will feed the hunger of their little souls for more than mere physical bread.

Shadow and Substance

As some enter into the joy of celebrating Passover as a family, community, or congregation, a common reaction from those not accustomed to keeping the Feasts is one of contempt and judgment arising out of fear and ignorance. Many 'mainstream Christians' fear that those who begin celebrating the Feasts of the Lord are falling back 'under the law' and losing their 'liberty in Christ'. We must love them where they are and give them no reason to justify their fear that we will turn legalistic and religiously prideful or self-righteous as we learn to live in submission to the Torah (Word of God). This is a real sand trap that the enemy sets for those beginning their wonderful journey into a Biblical

---

[2] Mah nishtana' is the recital of the traditional four questions by the youngest child at the seder table.

worship of the Lord. It is possible to forget, somewhere along the way, that we were all sinners saved by grace, and that we keep the commandments of God, not to earn our way into heaven, or to prove that we are better than those who don't, but out of a pure motive of love and devotion to God.

> **"For this is the love of God that we keep His commandments."** (1 John 5:3)

But they also, despite their fears, are not to judge those who choose to keep the Feasts of the Lord rather than man-made celebrations rooted in paganism.

The Word says,

> **"Let no one judge you in food or in drink, or regarding a festival or a new moon or Sabbaths, which are a shadow of things to come, but the substance is of Messiah."** (Col. 2:16-17)

We should at least have liberty in Messiah to walk in obedience to the commandments of God and to celebrate His feasts, in full recognition that these are a shadow (or contain symbols) of the 'Real Thing' that is – the Messiah Yeshua! Perhaps one day we will no longer celebrate the Feasts when the Messiah lives and dwells amongst us here on earth (although I doubt it, since when the Lord returns and defeats the enemies of Israel, the first thing He commands is for all nations to celebrate the Feast of Tabernacles! Zech. 14:16) But for now, since He has ascended to heaven and sits at the right hand of the Father, we have only left with us the shadows and the Holy Spirit to guide us. But even a shadow has great benefit. When Peter's shadow fell upon people, they experienced healing.

> "...so that they brought the sick out into the streets and laid them on beds and couches, that at least the shadow of Peter passing by might fall on some of them...and they were all healed." (Acts 5:15-16)

If the shadow of Peter passing by could heal the multitudes, how much more so the shadow of the Savior of the world! So may we find healing when we allow the shadow of the Messiah to fall upon us by celebrating the festivals which all contain the shadow of which the substance is the Messiah.

CHAPTER NINE

PARALLEL IMAGES

How does the Passover reveal the Messiah? We may study the Biblical account of the exodus and the Passover service (Seder) itself to see all the amazing parallel images.

Choose a Lamb

> **"On the tenth of this month every man shall take for himself a lamb, according to the house of his father, a lamb for a household."** (Ex. 12:3)

It was exactly on the tenth day of this month that Yeshua rode into Jerusalem to present himself as the chosen Lamb of God. In keeping with the humble circumstances of His birth, He rode into Jerusalem on a donkey, in fulfillment of the Messianic Prophecy,

> **"Tell the daughter of Zion (Bat Tzion),**
> **'Behold, your King is coming to you,**
> **Lowly, and sitting on a donkey,**
> **A colt, the foal of a donkey."**
> (Zech 9:9; Matt. 21:5)

When Yeshua rode into the city of Jerusalem, the people waved palm branches and sang hallel[1] praises. Their desire was for a Messiah who would save them from their circumstances, their oppression. The people looked to a Messiah they hoped would rule and reign as King in perfect justice and righteousness; one who would bring perfect peace and joy to the earth. Even today, many Jewish people will not accept Yeshua as Messiah because 'He didn't bring peace to earth'. But what they didn't realize then, just as they still do not realize today, is that the Messiah needed to first fulfill His role as a suffering servant who would be led 'like a lamb to the slaughter' to save our souls, in fulfillment of the scriptures (Is. 53:7), before He could come to rule as the King of Kings, the Lion of the tribe of Judah. The lion and lamb - two faces of Messiah. He has already come to fulfill His role as the sacrificial Lamb; and we await His return as the triumphant 'Lion-King.'

A Lamb For a Household

The lamb was to be chosen for a household, not an individual. Scriptures give some evidence that our faith in Yeshua can also bring salvation to our whole households.

When a great earthquake supernaturally set Paul and Silas free from prison, the guard in astonishment asked, "What must I do to be saved?"

> **"So they said, "Believe on the Lord Yeshua the Messiah, and you will be saved, you and your household."** (Acts 16:31)

Noah, the only righteous man on earth was saved from the flood; he and his household. When the angels warned Lot (and

---

[1] Hallel is the Hebrew word for praise as in hallelu-yah (praise Yah).

even pulled him by the arm) to escape the wrath of God upon Sodom and Gomorrah, his whole household was also given an opportunity to flee. Only the sons-in-laws' mockery of Lot and his wife's disobedience in looking backwards caused them to forfeit their salvation.

The faith of a husband or wife can sanctify and make holy an unbelieving wife or husband and the children of their union.

> **"For the unbelieving husband is sanctified (m'kadesh) by the wife, and the unbelieving wife is sanctified by the husband; otherwise your children would be unclean, but now they are holy (kadushim)."** (1 Cor. 7:14)

Let us apply the blood of the Lamb of God, by faith, not only for ourselves, but for the salvation of our entire households!

A Lamb Without Blemish

> **"Your lamb shall be without blemish.. Now you shall keep it until the fourteenth day of the same month."** (Ex. 12:5-6)

Just as the lamb was to be inspected and watched over for four days to prove it was without spot or blemish, so was Yeshua inspected for these four days until Pilate pronounced him without any guilt or fault whatsoever. He said to them,

> **"I find no fault in Him."** (John 18:38)

The New Testament affirms that the precious blood of the Messiah, the Lamb without blemish, redeemed us.

> "Knowing that you were not redeemed with corruptible things, like silver or gold, from your aimless conduct received by tradition from your fathers, but with the precious blood of Messiah, as of a lamb without blemish and without spot."
> (1 Pet. 1:18-19)

Why did the lamb have to be without blemish? As a picture of the Messiah, the Passover Lamb of God, only a perfect sacrifice would suffice. Yeshua, the son of God, was tempted as we are on this earth, and yet He did not sin. Because of His obedience, even unto death, we can appropriate unto ourselves, by faith in the blood of the Lamb, the righteousness of God.

> "For He made Him who knew no sin to be sin for us, that we might become the righteousness of God in Him." (2 Cor. 5:21)

The Lamb That Was Slain

> "Now you shall keep it until the fourteenth day of the same month. Then the whole assembly of the congregation of Israel shall kill it at twilight."
> (Ex. 12:6)

Can you imagine your household taking in an adorable, innocent lamb for four whole days? Perhaps the children would be sent out several times a day to feed and water the pretty lamb. I am sure that if they are anything like my children, with a natural love for animals, especially the babies, they just wouldn't be able to resist petting the sweet thing a time or two in those four days. Can we imagine the children's horror when that same lamb, which they had grown to love, would be killed?

Why would God give such strange instructions to His people? Why on earth would it be the blood of an innocent lamb that would be the sign of salvation upon the Israelite households? It was in order to give a vivid word picture of the coming Messiah who would be, as a lamb led to the slaughter.

> **"He was oppressed and**
> **He was afflicted,**
> **Yet He opened not His mouth;**
> **He was led as a lamb to the slaughter,**
> **And as a sheep before it**
> **shearers is silent,**
> **So He opened not His mouth."**
> (Is. 53:7)

He Opened Not His Mouth

Yeshua, in fulfillment of these Messianic prophecies, also remained silent and did not open His mouth in self-defense. When the High-Priest (Cohen HaGadol) asked Yeshua for an answer to the false testimony of which some men accused Him, He did not answer.

> **"Yeshua remained silent and gave no answer."**
> (Mark 14:61)

> **"But Yeshua kept silent."** (Matt. 26:63)

> **"But He answered him not one word, so that the governor marveled greatly."** (Matt. 27:14)

Crucify Him!

Yeshua, according to all the gospel accounts, was handed over to the Gentiles, mocked, beaten, spat upon, and then killed (Luke 18:32). It was in God's perfect timing, exactly at the moment the lambs were being killed, that Yeshua was also nailed to an execution stake. This occurred on the Day of Preparation, before the first day of the Feast,

> **"Now it was the Preparation Day of the Passover, and about the sixth hour. And he said to them, "Here is your King!". But they cried out, "Away with Him, away with Him! Crucify Him!"**
> (John 19:14-15)

CHAPTER TEN

MESSIANIC PROPHECIES FULFILLED IN YESHUA

The Psalms of the Old Testament predicted Yeshua's crucifixion and describe many of its gruesome details:

> "...a band of evil men has encircled me, they have pierced my hands and my feet. I can count all my bones; people stare and gloat over me. They divide my garments among them and cast lots for my clothing." (Ps. 22:16-18)

In fact, they did divide up Yeshua's garments and cast lots for it.

> "Then they crucified Him, and divided His garments, casting lots, that it might be fulfilled which was spoken by the prophet..." (Matt. 27:35)

Eli, Eli, Lamah Azavtani?

The Psalmist, David, predicted Yeshua's final plea when he wrote,

> **"My God, My God, why have You forsaken Me? Why are You so far from helping me, and from the words of my groaning?"** (Ps. 22:1)

In Yeshua's final moments on the cross, He cried out in pain – not only the physical pain of the torturous execution, but one even perhaps more painful – that of a broken heart. For a brief moment, Abba (Father) turned His face away from His Son (Ben), and it was this excruciating abandonment that caused Yeshua to cry out, "Eli, Eli, lamah azvatani?", which translates in English,

> **"My God, my God, why have you forsaken Me?"** (Matt. 27:46)

I Will Never Leave Nor Forsake You

One of God's most wonderful promises to us in the Bible is that He will "never leave us and never forsake us." Most of us have experienced the pain of abandonment at some point in our lives. People may let us down; no one is there for us when we need help. There are times when it feels as if God also has abandoned us, we cannot see, feel, or hear Him. These are the times when we must know that Yeshua took all this agony of abandonment upon Himself on the cross, in order that we may be healed. Are you getting this? We have someone who will never, ever, leave or forsake us, no matter what. This is a promise we can count on.

> **"And if God is for us, who can be against us?"** (Rom. 8:31)

Vinegar to Drink

The Psalms even predict Yeshua's thirst on the cross and their giving Him vinegar to drink.

> "Reproach has broken my heart, and I am full of heaviness; I looked for someone to take pity, but there was none; and for comforters, but I found none. They also gave me gall for my food, and for my thirst they gave me vinegar to drink."
> (Ps. 69: 20-21)

Have you ever been in such a bad way and could find no one to take pity on you; no one to offer you comfort? Yeshua understands how we feel. He has experienced more rejection and mistreatment than we ever will in a lifetime!

> "They gave Him sour wine mingled with gall to drink. But when He had tasted it, He would not drink…Immediately one of them ran and took a sponge, filled it with sour wine and put it on a reed, and offered it to Him to drink." (Matt. 27:34, 48)

It Is Finished

As soon as Yeshua received the sour wine, He said, "It is finished!" (John 19:30) He then bowed His head and gave up His spirit. In the Hebrew, Yeshua said, "Nishlam!". As you can see, this word shares the same root as 'shalom': sh-l-m (שלם), which carries the meaning of peace, perfection, completeness, or wholeness. What was brought to completion? The complex and temporary system of animal sacrifices had come to an end. Yeshua had perfectly fulfilled the Messianic prophecies required for Him to take away the sins of the world as the Passover lamb. The Hebrew word, 'l'shalem' also means 'to pay'. When Yeshua said, 'Nishlam', He also confirmed that He has paid the full price, the complete ransom for our sins.

> **"For there is one God and one Mediator between God and men, the Man-Messiah Yeshua, who gave Himself a ransom for all..."** (1 Tim. 2:5-6)

The Veil Has Been Torn

At the moment Yeshua died, the curtain of the temple was torn in two from top to bottom (Matt. 27:51). Up until this time, this curtain or veil had acted as a divider between the people and the Most Holy place, where only the Cohen HaGadol (High Priest) could enter, and then only once a year on Yom Kippur (the Day of Atonement).

What, then, did the tearing of the veil at this time signify? The way into the presence of God in His most holy place, the way of intimacy with our Creator, Elohim, YHVH (hvhy) had now been opened to His people who could come boldly through the blood of the Lamb. This is not the old way through animal sacrifices, but a new and living way:

> **"Therefore, brethren, having boldness to enter the Holiest by the blood of Yeshua, by a new and living way which He consecrated for us, through the veil, that is, His flesh..."** (Heb. 10:19-20)

This is why Yeshua said, *"I am the Way...."* And why His followers were called 'People of the Way." After Yeshua's final sacrifice, we must now go through Him to The Father.

> "I am the way, the truth, and the life. No one comes to the Father except through Me." (John 14:6)

Not a Broken Bone

One specific instruction regarding the Passover Lamb was that none of its bones were to be broken. (Ex.12:46; Num. 9:12) In fulfillment of this scripture, none of Yeshua's bones were broken either.

> "The soldiers therefore came and broke the legs of the first man who had been crucified with Yeshua, and then those of the other. But when they came to Yeshua and found that he was already dead, they did not break his legs…These things happened so that the scripture would be fulfilled, 'Not one of His bones will be broken.'" (John 19:32-37)

A Bone of Contention

Speaking of bones, a different bone of contention and possible source of confusion and division surrounds the matter of the timing of the crucifixion. Some scriptures seem to indicate that Yeshua had already celebrated the Passover Seder with His disciple's the night before His crucifixion. Was this really a Passover meal? Did they slay their lamb a day ahead of time? Was this just a 'final teaching meal', as some claim, held the night before Passover? I would highly doubt it, as Yeshua specifically stated that they were preparing for and observing the Passover that night. Some scriptures state that the day Yeshua and His disciples prepared for the Passover was the first day of the feast of Unleavened Bread (Matt. 26:17). Then others, state that it was the next day, when He

Messianic Prophecies Fulfilled in Yeshua

was crucified, that was the Day of Preparation (the day before the Feast) (John 19:31). Well then, how may all these inconsistencies be reconciled, and is it possible that the gospel accounts contradict one another?

You weren't holding your breath for the answers, were you? I hope not!

These questions come up year after year by those who diligently seek the scriptures for clear-cut answers. And for those who like black and white, and who had hoped I could clear up the confusion in this matter, I'm afraid I will sorely disappoint you. I have studied the scriptures in this area up and down and sideways and I must confess, I still have not been able to reconcile the inconsistencies, even within the same gospel! Does this mean that I doubt Yeshua is the appointed Lamb of God who died for my sins? Not a chance! It's not that I'm trying to avoid the issue or pass the buck, but it seems to me that this is an area where even scholars fear to tread. Those who have made an attempt seem to contradict one another as well, and I certainly do not want to add to the fray. However, I would like to make a couple of comments:

First of all, it is a favorite tactic of anti-missionaries to point out inconsistencies in the New Testament, to place doubts in Believers' minds about the authenticity of Yeshua as the Messiah. What they discretely do not mention, however, is that the Old Testament also contains inconsistencies. One such example is found in the Book of Esther: In chapter 9, verse 10, it states that they killed Haman's ten sons. In the same chapter, verse 13, Esther's request is that they hang Haman's ten sons. How can they hang them if they have already been killed? There are several other examples, which are well documented. Does this mean that we discount the Old Testament? Of course not! We must keep in mind that in a piece of writing, thousands of years old, certain details may have been changed. Perhaps the human factor of the writer enters into play at times. There could be circumstances that we are not aware of, contextual issues, translation issues. The same holds true for the New Testament. We are also dealing with a period of time when the Temple and its services still existed; we may not be clear on exactly how the Passover was observed at this time. Passover and the Feast of Unleavened Bread, although considered almost one and the same now, were actually two separate Feasts. All these things combine to make the study difficult, especially if we are of melancholy temperament or intellectual persuasion where we have difficulties with non-absolutes. But many things of faith remain mysteries until the time God chooses to unveil them to us.

We can make things very complicated and confusing to the point of frustration and division, even leading to doubts about our faith. But if we keep the 'main thing' as the main thing, then we are going to make it through to the end. The 'main thing' is that Yeshua allowed Himself to be crucified in order to make atonement for our sins.

It was for our transgressions and iniquities that He was wounded and bruised: This is what the Hebrew prophet Isaiah, predicted hundreds of years before Yeshua's life, death, and resurrection:

> **"Surely He has borne our grief and carried our sorrows; yet we esteemed Him stricken, smitten by God, and afflicted. But He was wounded for our transgressions, He was bruised for our iniquities; the chastisement for our peace was upon Him, and by His stripes** (the lashes of the whip upon His back) **we are healed."** (Is. 53:4-5)

Just as the Cohen HaGadol (High Priest) of ancient days

would lay the iniquities of the children of Israel upon the head of the 'scapegoat' (azazel), so has the

> **"Lord laid on Him the iniquity of us all."** (Is. 53:6)

He was, as the prophet predicts,

> **"Cut off from the land of the living...stricken for the transgressions of His people."** (Is. 53:8)

> **"They made His grave with the wicked but with the rich at His death."** (Is. 53:9)

Yeshua fulfilled this scripture when he was crucified between two criminals, but laid in the tomb of a rich man from Arimathea, named Joseph (Matt. 27:38, 57-60).

Isaiah 53: The Controversy

This 53rd chapter of Isaiah is very important then, to reveal the role of the Messiah to us. Philip began at exactly these scriptures to preach Jesus to the eunuch. (Acts 8:32-35) We commissioned a scribe in Israel, a Jewish Believer, to calligraphy this chapter in Hebrew onto a parchment that we have framed for display in our living room. Unfortunately, this critical 'piece of the puzzle' is withheld from most Jewish people. It is not found in any of the 'siddur' books (prayer books) in the synagogues. Also the Torah portions that are read each Sabbath, even if one can comprehend the rapid-fire Hebrew chanting of the parashah and haftorah (traditional Sabbath scripture portions), we will never hear these scriptures being read in the synagogue – even if we attend faithfully each and every week. Why not? They are omitted! The readings skip from Isaiah 52 to Isaiah 54. Several other Messianic prophecies are also omitted from the readings. Is this a conspiracy? Perhaps... Catholic priests also tried to withhold the scriptures from the common people. It seems as if the religious leaders usually have too much at stake to risk upsetting the status quo. Even in Yeshua's day, the common people amongst the Jewish population loved him and listened attentively to His teachings. It was only the religious leaders who wanted to destroy Him out of jealousy and pride. They knew that they risked starting a riot if they were to openly apprehend Yeshua during the Feast! (Matt.26:5)

And today, the Jewish religious leaders are still greatly threatened by Yeshua, to such an extent that they withhold the scriptures that speak of Him most directly. Oh yes, I am well aware of the history of bloodshed, hatred, and persecution of the Jewish people by the so-called Christian Church. I have relatives who are holocaust survivors. I understand that part of the reaction against Yeshua is because of the sins of Christian Fathers of the faith and their disciples. But we must not hold Yeshua accountable for sins that He did not commit, even if those who claimed to be His followers did these terrible things in His name. If someone stole my cheque book and wrote a whole mess of bad cheques and forged my signature to do so, the crime is theirs and not mine, even if they are my so-called friends. (With friends like these, who needs enemies?)

The truth is that most Rabbinical scholars, as least before their anti-Yeshua reaction, agreed that these scriptures refer to a personal Messiah, a suffering servant who would give His life in exchange for our souls. No matter what we think of Yeshua, we owe it to people to give them the information (especially when written by our own Hebrew prophets), and let intelligent people think for themselves. It is God who blinded the eyes of the Jewish people (Is. 6:9-10, John 12:39), and it is He who is now lifting that blindness so that many Jewish people are seeing Yeshua as their

Passover Lamb. Is it possible that it is now time for you to obtain a copy of the Bible and read it for yourself? Maybe you'd like to start with the prophetic book of Isaiah, chapter 53!

CHAPTER ELEVEN

THE BLOOD

> **"Now the blood shall be a sign for you on the houses where you are. And when I see the blood, I will pass over you; and the plague shall not be on you to destroy you when I strike the land of Egypt."** (Ex. 12:13)

Blood is not a subject we usually like to discuss. Blood……. yuck! Most of us have a natural abhorrence to blood. A woman is considered ritually unclean (Biblically) during the time of her monthly menstrual flow.

> **"If a woman has a discharge, and the discharge from her body is blood, she shall be set apart seven days; and whoever touches her shall be unclean until evening."** (Lev. 15:19)

Intercourse between husband and wife during this time is expressly forbidden. People who follow God and His word are forbidden to eat any blood. It must be drained from all the meat that we eat in order to be 'kosher'. I remember my mother breaking each egg into a little bowl before adding to the big mixing bowl. This was, "just in case of any blood spots", she explained. What is the big deal about blood? The Word of God explains this to us:

> **"For the life of the flesh is in the blood, and I have given it to you upon the altar to make atonement for your souls; for it is the blood that makes atonement for the soul."** (Lev. 17:11)

Although this is often not taught in Sunday (or Shabbat) nursery school classes, it is the blood that makes atonement for our souls. For this reason, blood is a very precious commodity. It is also the basis for the blood sacrifices which God commanded the people of Israel to offer up to Him at the Temple, along with specific and rigid instructions on exactly how to do so.

Obedience Rather Than Sacrifice

The prophets often had a controversy with the priests over these sacrifices. They claimed that to sin, and then to simply offer up the blood sacrifice with a 'wrong heart', was to miss the whole point – that God desires obedience, righteousness and justice rather than empty sacrifice.

> **"For I desire mercy, not sacrifice, and acknowledgement of God rather than burnt offerings."** (Hos. 6:6)

> **"To do righteousness and justice is more acceptable to the Lord than sacrifice."** (Prov. 21:3)

And yet, it was God Himself who instituted the system of blood sacrifices. The New Testament contains the same principle. Some people believe that Christianity teaches a doctrine of salvation by faith, in which 'works' or behavior is irrelevant. This is a false doctrine. The Old and New Testaments are consistent and harmonize one with another. The Israelites were saved by faith in the blood of the lamb, just as are we who believe in Yeshua, saved by faith and not by works. I once remarked to my mother in a late night 'Passover conversation' that the angel of death did not knock on each door to see if the ones inside had given enough to charity, or had been a good baba (grandmother) that year! Their salvation depended completely upon God's grace and their faith in applying the blood of the lamb that was slain. And yet God would shortly lead them, through Moses, to Mt. Sinai, to receive the Torah (the law) that they were expected to obey. To sin is to transgress the law (Torah). To those Christians who believe that the law (Torah) is irrelevant because of their faith, we need to keep in mind that the New Testament contains these words:

> **"Do we make void the law (Torah) through faith? Certainly not! On the contrary, we establish the law."** (Rom. 3:31)

> **"What then? Shall we sin because we are not under law but under grace? Certainly not!"** (Rom. 6:15)

Just as the Israelites made the mistake of offering up the blood sacrifice to God while still indulging in willful sin, so do some Christians offer up the blood of Yeshua as their 'guilt offering', while continuing in sin. This is still unacceptable to God and insults the Spirit of grace. The blood of Yeshua will not cover willful, unrepentant sin:

> **"For if we sin willfully after we have received the knowledge of the truth, there no longer remains a sacrifice for sins, but a certain fearful expectation of judgment, and fiery indignation which will devour the adversaries."** (Heb. 10:26-27)

The issue of the blood sacrifice is not an either / or matter.

Yeshua, as both Cohen (priest) and Navi (prophet), understood the importance of both the blood and obedience. Obedience is an expected natural by-product of our gratitude for our salvation by grace through faith in the blood of the lamb. Faith and works should go hand and hand in our lives as Believers. One without the other is dead, useless, of no profit to anyone:

> **"For as the body without the spirit is dead, so faith without works is dead also."**
> (James 2:26)

And You Shall Apply It

It must have taken a monumental leap of faith for the Israelites to kill the lambs. How on earth could blood protect them from spiritual forces of darkness, they must have wondered. And yet it would not have been enough for them to simply believe. They needed to also apply the blood to their doorposts (mezuzot)[1] and lintels of their homes.

> **"And you shall take a bunch of hyssop, dip it in the blood that is in the basin, and strike the lintel and the two doorposts with the blood that is in the basin."** (Ex. 12:22a)

It is also not enough for us to just 'believe' in Yeshua. Many people believe in Him, and yet have not personally applied His blood, symbolically, to the lintels and doorposts of their lives. Yeshua said that even the demons believe that there is one God....

---

1 Mezuzot – plural for mezuzah – Hebrew word for doorpost, but also for the little box containing a selection of scripture verses that most Jewish people affix to their doorposts in obedience to the commandment. (Deut. 6:9)

so what! (James 2:19). The fruit of our belief and the application of the blood to our 'mezuzot' should be a release from slavery and from darkness and a binding of us forever to the Lord. The mezuzah (doorpost) was a significant place in the household. This is where the Lord has directed us to write His commandments.

> **"And you shall write them on the doorposts of your house and on your gates"** (Deut. 11:20)

It is also here, where if a slave loved his master and did not want to go free from him after his time of service was complete, he would pierce his ear with an awl to the doorpost, signifying his pledge of lifetime obedience and service to his master (Ex. 21:4). Now that Yeshua has set us free from the kingdom of darkness and from slavery to sin, we are to voluntarily pierce our ear to the mezuzah of the kingdom of righteousness. We are now slaves of God and righteousness.

> **"But now having been set free from sin, and having becomes slaves of God, you have your fruit to holiness, and the end, everlasting life."** (Rom. 6:22)

Staying Under the Blood

> **"And none of you shall go out of the door of his house until morning."** (Ex. 12:22b)

It is clear from the Passover that God required the Israelites to remain under the covering of the blood in order to be spared. Had they left that covering and walked the streets of Egypt, their firstborns would have been struck down in just the same way as the Egyptians. We cannot 'walk the streets of Egypt', conforming to the ways of the world its lifestyle, idolatry, and lack of morality and still expect to be safe. We must be careful to stay under the covering of the covenant of the blood of the Lamb by aspiring to live a life of holiness. The Lord asks us to 'be holy as He is Holy' and we are assured that

> **"Without holiness no one will see the Lord."**
> (Heb. 12:14)

Egypt not only represents a physical nation; it also stands for the 'world system'. "Israel and Egypt represent two different world-conceptions, two ways of looking at God and Man that are not merely in conflict, but mutually exclusive."[2]

We cannot live our lives with one foot in each world. We must make a clear decision to 'come out of her', or to risk sharing in her sins and receiving of her plagues.

> **"Come out of her, my people, lest you share in her sins, and lest you receive of her plagues."**
> (Rev. 18:4)

Doorway of Life

When the blood has been applied to the lintel and doorposts, it forms a certain Hebrew letter: chet {ח}. This stands for life (chai) {חי}, which means 'life'. Those who remained under this doorway of blood were safe from the wrath of God that fell upon the Egyptians.

---

[2] Pentateuch & Haftorahs, *'Israel and Egypt: The Spiritual Contrast'*, Hebrew Text English Translation & Commentary, The Soncino Press, Edited by Dr. J.H. Hertz, pg. 396.

> "For the Lord (יהוה) will pass through to strike the Egyptians; and when He sees the blood on the lintel and on the two doorposts, the Lord will pass over the door and not allow the destroyer to come into your houses to strike you." (Ex. 12:23)

This scripture tells us something very important about God: The destroyer is under His command. He is not somebody to mess with!

The blood of the Lamb is the only thing powerful enough to protect us from the wrath of God. When He sees the blood, He will 'pass over' us. This is where the name Passover comes from. Every time we celebrate Passover, we should breathe a mighty sigh of relief that through the blood of the Lamb, the destroyer will pass-over us.

The blood of Yeshua also forms a doorway of blood that leads to salvation and life. The gospels are called the Good News. But I think they should rather be called the Good News and the Bad News (which one do you want first?).

THE GOOD NEWS - AND THE BAD..

Not Appointed to Wrath

O.K. here is the 'good news' first:

> "He who believes in the Son has everlasting life..." (John 3:36)

And here comes the bad:

> "...and he who does not believe the son shall not see life, but the wrath of God abides on him." (John 3:36)

The wrath of God is something I don't even want to contemplate. People seem to be eagerly anticipating the coming of the Lord. But the scriptures call it a 'dreadful day' (Mal. 4:5). I just thank God that in His mercy He sent Yeshua, so that I could take cover under the shelter of His blood. God does not take pleasure in death or destruction; but He cannot allow violence, wickedness, and corruption to reign on this earth forever. And so He has provided a way out for us; God Himself provided the lamb. Through Him, we are not subject to wrath.

> **"For God did not appoint us to wrath, but to obtain salvation through our Lord Yeshua the Messiah."**
> (1 Thess. 5:9)

And yet, God did not make us little robots or automatons; He gave us a free will. Although He calls us, and His Holy Spirit woos us, it is still up to us to make the choice to receive this gift of salvation through Yeshua or to leave ourselves open to face the wrath of God. We can see however, what happened to the Egyptians. I think the choice should be an easy one....

The Coming Lion of Judah

Throughout God's Word, the prophets foretold of His coming wrath upon the earth. Yeshua is returning, not as the meek, sacrificial lamb, but as the mighty Lion of Yehudah (Judah), to execute judgment upon the peoples of the earth, especially upon the enemies of Israel.

> **"Come near, you goyim (nations), to hear; and heed, you people! Let the earth hear, and all that is in it, the world and all things that come forth from it. For the indignation of the Lord is against all**

> the goyim (nations), and His fury against all their armies; He has utterly destroyed them; He has given them over to the slaughter. Also, their slain shall be thrown out; their stench shall rise from their corpses and the mountains shall be melted with their blood." (Is. 34:1-3)

Yes, God is a merciful God and does not desire even one person to perish. Therefore, He has given each one of us the opportunity to place the blood of the Lamb, by faith, on the doorposts and lintels of our hearts, by receiving Yeshua's atonement for our sins. But we must not forget that God is also the God of the sword and of judgment. He is called 'Ish Milchamah', a man of war. (Ex. 15:3)

The Fate of the Gentile Believers in the Nations

> "Though I make a full end of all nations where I have scattered you…" (Jer. 30:11)

What will happen to the covenant people of יהוה in these nations? Of course only God knows the future with a certainty, but if we look at the Passover story, we can see that God made a clear distinction between His covenant people Israel, and the Egyptians who were not in covenantal relationship with Him. Gentiles (the goyim) who were at one time not in covenantal relationship with the God of Israel have now been grafted into the Olive Tree, which is Israel, through the blood of the Messiah.

A Refuge

I've got a revelation for you – Jesus is not only for the Jews! He was slain as the Lamb of God for the whole world – for all of mankind! A definition for propitiation is 'appeasement of divine wrath'. We must receive it deep into our spirits that Yeshua has appeased the wrath of God and we may live at peace with Him, with ourselves and with others. When we fall, He is there to lift us up. He is a strong refuge to which we can always run when we are in distress, but when we are too weary to even run to Him, He is still faithful to gird us up from underneath. The following scripture that has brought me great comfort during those times when I have felt too weary, worn out or discouraged to even run to Him is:

> **"The eternal God is your refuge, and underneath are the everlasting arms."** (Deut. 33:27)

There may be coming a time when God will once again pour out His wrath and plagues upon the earth (Rev. 8-11). But we need not fear, for God will be then, as He was for His people in Egypt, a refuge in times of trouble.

> **"God is our refuge and strength, a very present help in trouble."** (Ps. 46:1)

CHAPTER TWELVE

PREPARING FOR PASSOVER

> **"Where do you want us to prepare for you to eat the Passover?"** (Matt. 26:17)

Celebrating the Passover requires preparation. Exactly what are the preparations that need to be made? The commandment in preparation to eat the Passover is to first cleanse our homes of any leaven (yeast). I find it almost comical, if it wasn't so sad, the lengths and depths and breadths that people will go to in their own doctrinal meanderings to circumvent the direct commandments of God. My son came home one day from a playing at a friend's house during Passover and said that they "don't get the yeast out of their homes; they just don't eat it." Some people lock up their leavened products in a special closet or cupboard. Some Jewish people even follow a custom of 'leasing' their leaven to Gentiles by signing a paper notarized by a rabbi and thus being able to keep it in their homes, since it doesn't 'belong' to them, and then 'buying it back' after Passover. But the Word of God is clear in this matter:

> **"On the first day you shall remove leaven from your houses. For whoever eats leavened bread from the first day until the seventh day, that person shall be cut off from Israel."** (Ex. 12:15)

Spring Cleaning

In traditional Jewish households, preparation for Passover begins long before the actual date (Nissan 14)[1], with an intensive and thorough 'spring cleaning' of the home. Every drawer, every cupboard, every shelf is emptied and cleaned and organized. Homes are cleared out of old, unwanted items. In Israel, where no real charitable organization exists for the widespread distribution of goods to the poor, items are merely set out by the garbage bins to be picked up by whoever needs or wants them. The saying "one man's garbage is another man's treasure" certainly hold true here! Many new immigrants (ourselves included) have furnished their entire apartments from their pickings at the garbage! The degree to which one 'spring cleans' their home before Passover probably depends on individual temperament, but almost everyone is busy to some extent with this task.

Traditional Custom vs. Biblical Command

We must keep in mind that when we discuss the preparation and celebration of Passover, a significant difference exists between traditional Jewish practice and Biblical command.

The only Biblical command is to cleanse our homes of yeast on the first day and to refrain from eating any food containing yeast for the entire seven days. Traditional, Orthodox Jewish customs however, are an entirely different matter! In my childhood home,

---

[1] Consult any Jewish calendar for the equivalent date for the 14th of Nissan. Because the Jewish calendar is lunar based, the corresponding date will differ somewhat each year.

we had an entirely new set of dishes, glasses, cutlery, bowls, pots and pans that were used strictly for Passover. Everything had to be cleansed – including the countertops and cupboards. All foods had to be specially stamped 'kosher for Passover', in case the regular food contained even a minute speck of yeast. In Israel, large containers of boiling water are set up on street corners for people to boil their dishes and utensils to render them 'kosher' for Passover. When I turned to the Lord and read what the Bible actually had to say, I embraced God's commands out of obedience, but have continued to reject many man made 'traditions of the elders'. Although some Messianic Jews who observe these Rabbinical customs would disagree with me, I believe that I have Yeshua's agreement in considering most of them an unnecessary burden.

I certainly observed the weight these man-made rules and regulations regarding the Passover as a burden on my mother's back that she found increasingly difficult to bear.

> **"For they bind heavy burdens, hard to bear, and lay them on men's shoulders..."** (Matt. 23:4)

Perhaps all these 'religious works' in preparation for the feast cause one to appear holy, but Yeshua sees through the façade. For holiness is more than religious ritual; it is an inward transformation of our hearts. Yeshua ran head-on into the contempt of the scribes and Pharisees who objected to the way Yeshua and his disciples refused to observe the 'traditions of the elders', particularly in the matter of ritual hand-washing. They asked,

> **"Why do your disciples transgress the tradition of the elders?"** (Matt. 15:2)

Yeshua replied by quoting from Isaiah:

"These people draw near to Me with their mouth, and honor Me with their lips, but their heart is far from Me and in vain they worship Me, teaching as doctrines the commandments of men." (Is. 29:13, Matt. 15:8-9)

Apparently, God Himself does not appreciate men making up their own rules and then trying to pass them off as divine commandments. Although we do not need to trash all traditions, for some are beautiful and rich in spiritual significance, we must keep in mind that they are merely tradition, not command. As the Fiddler on the Roof sang, "Tradition…tradition!" this has been the glue that has held the Jewish people together during their long period of exile from the Land. These traditions, therefore, are firmly entrenched in most Jewish people's minds and difficult to dislodge.

I recall my first Passover in the Land, being surprised by how strictly even secular Jews kept the Passover. I once offered a stick of gum to my next door neighbor's daughter, whom I know to be not at all 'religious'. She insisted on checking first if the gum had the kosher for Passover stamp. No amount of my explanation that gum doesn't contain yeast could persuade her otherwise. And so we may respect the faith of those who abide by the traditions of the elders, and yet know that we are not bound by the commandments of men, even if they are taught as doctrine of God.[2]

---

2 Some controversy exists over what exactly constitutes chametz (leaven). Sephardic (Eastern/African) Jews believe rice is permissible, while Ashkenazi Jews (originating in Europe) forbid the eating of rice during Passover. Some consider using flour or any leavening agents such as baking powder as taboo (but then I read, "leavening agents' on packages marked kosher for Passover, so – go figure….).

Cleaning the Chametz

We may cleanse our homes of every minute trace of yeast (chametz), and yet miss the whole point. The Bible tells us that chametz symbolizes sin. Yeshua said to beware the chametz (leaven) of the Pharisees and Sadducees (Matt. 16:6). He explained that He was not speaking of actual leaven in their bread, but of their false doctrines. He accused them of being hypocrites, blind men leading other blind men into the ditch, doing what they do to be noticed, to gain the praise of men; wanting the best seats, vying for visible places of honor and craving recognition, respected greetings, and titles attached to their names (Matt. 23:5-8). What is this sin Yeshua is describing where people want to impress others with outward appearances, titles, degrees or accomplishments? Have you ever been with someone who seems to seek your approval by drawing attention to themselves through mentioning the wonderful things they have done or said, the 'important' people that they know, or even who THEY have led to the Lord? Did you begin to feel somewhat uncomfortable by their not-so-subtle boasting in themselves or their 'name dropping'? I believe it is because our spirits immediately pick up on the sin of pride and find it distasteful. It's like taking a bite of some appealing looking food and then upon recognizing its offensive taste, looking for a discrete way to spit it out! Sin, and especially pride, is an offensive stench in the nostrils of God. It is the sin of pride that brought down Satan[3], the light bearer, from an honored place in the presence of God to be flung to the earth by boasting,

"I will be like the Most High" (Is. 14:14)

Just as a little yeast causes the whole lump of dough to rise,

---

[3] In this Hebrew scripture Satan, or Lucifer, as it is often wrongly translated, is called 'Hallel ben shachar' - literally 'praise son of the dawn'. (Is.14:12)

so does a little pride cause us to act 'puffed up'; whereas we are to walk 'humbly before our God' and not to think more highly of ourselves than we ought. The apostle Paul used the analogy of chametz (leaven) to rebuke the Corinthian Church over their sin of pride.

> **"Your glorying is not good. Do you not know that a little leaven leavens the whole lump? Therefore purge out the old leaven, that you may be a new lump, since you truly are unleavened."** (1 Cor. 5:6-7)

Indeed, the cleansing of our homes from yeast is only a symbol of what is really to take place in preparation for Passover – a purging of the revealed malice and wickedness that continues to dwell within us.

> **"For indeed Messiah, our Passover, was sacrificed for us. Therefore let us keep the feast, not with old leaven, nor with the leaven of malice and wickedness, but with the unleavened bread of sincerity and truth."** (1 Cor. 5:7-8)

In the Hebrew, a related word chamutz actually means 'sour', as in a 'sour cucumber (pickle) or vinegar; or anything corrupted or rotten. We need to rid ourselves of anything rotten or corrupt that is making our lives 'sour'.

The Candle and the Feather

It is truly only the Holy Spirit that can transform us from within; we cannot change ourselves without the illumination of the Light of God. Before Yeshua came to live inside of me and the Spirit of God came to dwell with me, exchanging my hard heart of stone to a heart of flesh, I strived in vain to change myself. I indulged in destructive habit patterns that kept me chained to a cycle of defeat; my explosive temper damaged the tender spirit of my young children, as I struggled under the pressures of being a single mother alone in the world. But when Yeshua came into my life and my heart, the Spirit of God miraculously set me free from many, many of these things. Some changes came immediately, while others are still being worked out in my life. But this I know,

> **"He who has begun a good work in us will complete it in Messiah Yeshua!"** (Phil. 1:6)

Sometimes progress seems slow, but just as a child cannot see themselves growing, so too can we not always 'see' our spiritual growth until we reach some landmark. A children's songwriter and performer sings, *"I wonder if I'm growing...my Mom says yes I'm growing, but I'm hardly bigger at all."* In the song, the child doesn't really believe Mom that he's growing until he realizes he can finally reach the sink. Almost every day, our then two-year-old daughter Liat, played at the neighborhood park in Jerusalem. She saw the children drink from the fountain, but she could not reach the water without help from Mom – until one day…..one proud day she was able to push the button and drink from the fountain herself! My son has been going through a growth spurt. You can almost visibly see him growing and filling out in form. Many of us parents mark our children's height on the wall so that we can track their growth. Sometimes growth is slow and other times it is quick; but unless some catastrophe interferes, we rest confidently in the fact that our children will grow and develop. So too, by the transforming power of the Holy Spirit will we be changed from glory to glory into the image of His son.

This truth is beautifully illustrated in the traditional Jewish ceremony called 'b'dikat chametz' (checking for yeast). As I mentioned earlier, every year on the evening before Passover, my mother would dim the lights in the house and we would follow closely behind my father, holding a feather and a candle, searching the house for any hidden pieces of bread. My mother had hidden several pieces ahead of time in nooks and crannies of each room and we children excitedly hollered and jumped and pointed as the light of the candle exposed each crumb of leaven. Although we always had fun and enjoyed this custom, we had no idea why we did such a thing, besides the fact that it was a part of Passover. It wasn't until I became a Believer in Yeshua that the Holy Spirit revealed the true significance of this ancient ceremony. The candle represents the light of God, or Yeshua, the Light of the World, which shines in the dark places of our hearts to reveal hidden 'leaven' (sin). The feather represents the wings of the Holy Spirit, who appeared over Yeshua at his mikvah as a dove. It is the ministry of the Holy Spirit that sweeps this sin out of our inner beings with a gentle brush of His wings. No matter how hard we try, we either fail to transform ourselves in our own strength, or fail to see the sin in the first place. God in His infinite mercy, both reveals our sin and cleanses us from its influence upon our lives. We may find sin coming to the surface in our lives in the period before Passover that we didn't even know still lurked within. This is distressing. Perhaps we considered these issues in our lives already 'dealt with', forgiven, healed – and there they are again! We hate it and so do those around us who see these sins manifesting. But there is hope! Sin can only dwell in the darkness where it lives and grows. Yeast thrives best in moist, dark, concealed places of the body. But exposed to the Light, confessed sin cannot survive.

> **"He who covers his sins will not prosper, but whoever confesses and forsakes them will have mercy."** (Prov. 28:13)

Once the pieces of leavened bread are collected in the bag or basket, they are taken out of the home and burned. This symbolizes the complete destruction of these sins and the breaking of their hold on us. Halleluyah! The children (especially boys) love a bonfire and look forward each year to the burning of the chametz. Unfortunately one year when we lived in a top floor apartment, our son began the chametz bonfire on the balcony – a practice I would not recommend you try at home!

Boasting Against the Branches

One of the areas of pride in the Christian Church that Paul warned against is towards the Jewish people. It might be tempting to develop an attitude of superiority if one believes, "I am saved; you are not…I know the truth and have the answers but you do not." But the apostle Paul warns Gentiles not to 'boast against the (natural) branches', but to remember that it is not the Gentile Christian Church that supports the root, but the (Jewish) root supports the Church! (Rom. 11:17-18). Without a proper understanding of God's plan for the Jewish people, the Church, and all of humanity, it is all too easy for the Church to fall into the sin of pride, arrogance, and conceit.

> **"For I do not desire, brethren, that you should be ignorant of this mystery, lest you should be wise in your own opinion, that blindness in part has happened to Israel until the fullness of the Gentiles has come in. And so all Israel will be saved, as it is written:"** (Rom. 11:25-26)

The blindness upon Israel with regards to their own Messiah is all part of God's perfect plan – in order that the fullness of the Gentiles be harvested into the kingdom. This realization should be enough to turn arrogance into gratitude. For salvation is of the Jews. The Christian Church owes a great debt to the Jewish people for their salvation in the Messiah, for a place in the Covenant of promise and for the Word of God itself that the Jewish people preserved over the centuries at great sacrifice.

The Sin of Ingratitude

When a new king arose over Egypt, 'who knew not Joseph', the Egyptians oppressed, afflicted, and enslaved the Israelites. How soon did Egypt forget its debt of gratitude towards Joseph for saving so many of their kinsmen! But ingratitude is part of our sin nature. We all tend to forget at times, the good things others have done for us. The apostle Paul exhorts the Gentile church to repay the debt they owe the Jews by giving of their material resources in an expression of gratitude for the great spiritual blessings of the Messiah, the Bible, and salvation – all of which came through the Jewish people.

> **"It pleased them indeed, and they are their debtors. For if the Gentiles have been partakers of their** (the Jews') **spiritual things, their duty is also to minister to them in material things."** (Rom. 15:27)

How may this debt be repaid? It is through a material demonstration of giving to the Jews, but especially towards the household of faith. Many Churches engage in good works towards the poor and give to mission programs all over the world, and this is good. And yet many within the Gentile Church display negligence towards their debt owed to the Jewish people, showing ingratitude, arrogance, and even contempt instead. How much more could be accomplished for the Kingdom of God with regards to Israel if the Church would only remember her debt, and give as commanded in a spirit of gratitude and humility.

Without Love We Are Nothing

There is one other area of pride, especially amongst Torah observant Messianic congregations, which has become of personal concern to me. This is an anti-Church attitude that is expressed something like this, "I keep the Torah, you don't; I obey God's commandments and you don't. Therefore I am better than you are and stand at a higher level in God's estimation than you who remain in ignorance and sin towards keeping Torah and especially the Feasts." We must keep in mind the parable Yeshua told of the two men – one who prayed : "Thank you God that I am not like those sinners over there…" and the one who could not even lift his eyes heavenward, but kept his head bowed in shame and prayed, *"Abba, have mercy upon me, a sinner."* Which man was justified before the Lord? It was the man who humbly acknowledged his undeserving state before His God and still asked for mercy. We are all undeserving and saved by grace. We do not become more deserving of His grace and favor because we keep the feast of Passover. We keep the Feast as a response to His grace; not that we loved Him but He first loved us and chose us…As a loving and devoted wife does the things for her husband that she knows he loves and refrains from doing those things he hates, so we as the Bride, desire to behave in ways that please our Bridegroom. But if we do all things and yet do not have love, we are nothing (1 Cor. 13).

The message of the gospel is one of love. Yeshua said others would know we are His disciples by our love for one another (John 13:35). When asked which is the most important commandment, Yeshua gave a two-fold answer:

> "**Hear, O Israel, (יהוה) our God, (יהוה) is one. And you shall love the Lord your God with all your heart and with all your soul, with all your mind, and with all your strength. This is the first**

> **commandment. And the second, like it, is this: You shall love your neighbor as yourself. There is no other commandment greater than these."**
> (Mark 12:29-31)

Yes, our love for God is expressed by our obedience to His commandments (1 John 5:2-3). This is the first command. But the second command is 'like it' – to love our neighbor as ourselves. If we do not love our brothers and sisters, then we may think we are holy and righteous, walking in obedience and love towards God, but the truth is that we are still stumbling around blinded in the darkness (1 John 2:11). It is true that we have an obligation to warn others where they are walking in sin (Ezek. 3:21), but before trying to gouge the speck out of our brother's eye, we must truly notice and deal with the hefty planks in our own (Matt. 7: 3-6). I well understand that living according to one's convictions without causing offence to friends and family members, is often a difficult, if not impossible task. And others may interpret our stand for righteousness as a lack of love when we refuse to participate in their state of spiritual compromise or religious celebrations that we discover to be rooted in paganism. But still we must beware of the subtle development of a religious, self-righteous, judgmental attitude in ourselves towards those brothers and sisters who may be where we were spiritually, only a short time ago ourselves! How soon we forget. We must ask ourselves, and answer with painful honesty, if our religious activity has simply become a cover for a stony heart? We must beware of bitter roots growing in us that will cause much defilement and trouble in the Body of Messiah.

> **"See to it that no one misses the grace of God and that no bitter roots grow up to cause trouble and defile many."** (Heb. 12:15)

Better Check Your Pews

We like to start every congregational Seder by planting pieces of bread under the pews or chairs and then, after explaining the b'dikat chametz ceremony[4], asking the congregants to check their area for any chametz. Each one brings their symbolic piece of leaven up to the basket at the front and then we collectively pray over it that the Light of the World will shine into the dark places of our hearts to illuminate any hidden sin and that the Holy Spirit would then gently sweep it away and that it would be removed from us as far as the West is from the East. For we know our God is faithful to forgive confessed sin and to cleanse us from all iniquity.

> **"If we confess our sins, He is faithful and just to forgive us our sins and to cleanse us from all unrighteousness."** (1 John 1:9)

If we ever come to the place where we think we have no sin to confess, then we are really in trouble! For this shows us to be completely deceived by pride. Whoever says they have no sin is a liar (1 John 1:8). Let us bring all our sin to the Light, in a spirit of humility, and ask the Holy Spirit to cleanse us from all unrighteousness, that we may walk in a greater degree of freedom this Passover.

I include here my answer to a sister in the Lord's question about this practice of cleansing the yeast out of our homes.

1. Do you do the candle and feather tradition as a way to explain to the kids about Passover or do you really rid your house of yeast also? (I just bought a large bag at Costco) I have been trying (3 times 3 fails) to make the Challah. I was under

---

[4] The traditional ceremony of checking and cleansing the place of all leaven before Passover.

the impression that the feather and candle thing was a symbol. I was told that you actually go through your house and take a close look at your video's, books, toys and basically everything and make sure that it is pleasing to God and not evil. Am I missing the point? I understand the search of our hearts part.

A. I take the Bible quite literally. We get all the yeasted products out of the house. "Seven days you shall eat unleavened bread. On the first day you shall remove leaven from your houses. For whoever eats leavened bread from the first day until the seventh day, that person shall be cut off from Israel." (Ex. 12:15)

Yes, the candle and feather things is just symbolic. It is a teaching tool for the children about sin and getting it out of our lives. The yeast can be removed any old way, but the kids like the feather and candle. Yes, I definitely try to keep our home free of what the Bible calls "accursed things". These are the things which God calls "devoted to destruction". Items associated with the demonic realm, idols, magic, sorcery, (including Harry Potter and Halloween paraphenalia) New Age books, jewelry, etc. All these things bring the kingdom of darkness into our homes and opens a door to the enemy. Notice that Israel could not have victory or stand before their enemies until the accursed items were discovered and destroyed. This may be one of the reasons why some Christian families are having trouble and don't experience victory. They may be in possession of many items that should be destroyed. (Joshua 7:12) The Holy Presence of God cannot dwell in a defiled temple (including our dwelling places).

PART TWO

THE SEDER

CHAPTER THIRTEEN

PREPARING FOR THE SEDER

The Hagaddah

We now come to the point that we have all been eagerly waiting for – the Seder! The Hebrew word 'seder' means 'order'. A common reply in Israel when asked how you are doing is "b'seder", which literally means 'in order'. It means we're okay; everything is in place as it should be. The Passover Seder is simply a traditional way of bringing an order to the celebration of the feast: the eating of the matzah (unleavened bread), marror (bitter herbs) and lamb; the narrative of the Biblical account of our exodus from Egypt. The book used to follow a traditional Passover Seder is called a Hagaddah, which comes from the root, 'to tell'. These books are usually beautifully illustrated and give expression to the wonderful Jewish gifting in art, sometimes suppressed in Orthodox Jewish communities due to the fear of transgressing the commandment prohibiting the creation of 'images' in the Ten Commandments. The Hagaddah however, is simply a guide. There is no 'one way' of celebrating a Passover Seder. Since this is merely a tradition, we have liberty to modify and to accommodate the creativity of the Holy Spirit in each and every Seder. The traditional Jewish Hagaddah also does not emphasize the blood of the Passover lamb and certainly lacks the revelation of the Messiah in the Passover. Several Rabbinical stories from the

Talmud (oral law) and 'bubbamises' (Jewish fables) are included which some Messianics choose to avoid. For this reason, several gifted authors have created a 'Messianic Passover Hagaddah' that is available from several Messianic sources. These are helpful, but we must keep in mind, that they are also just a guide that may be adapted. For those who may be anxious about wanting to "do it right', I would say, "Fear not!". The basic commands are to cleanse the leaven from your homes, eat unleavened bread (matzah), bitter herbs (marror or horseradish) and the lamb, plus orally recount the Passover story, especially for the children. If you have done these things; if you have revealed Yeshua as the Passover lamb of God, you have fulfilled the command.

Who to Invite?

The Passover Seder is a wonderful outreach to both Jews and Gentiles alike. We have found it an incredible blessing to help guide sincere Christians through a Messianic Passover service. A congregational Passover Seder takes some organization, but is well worth it. And with prayer, the Holy Spirit is well able to seek out and find a lost sheep or two of Israel to bring back into green pastures through a Messianic Passover Seder as well. Usually, the Seder is a family celebration (a lamb per household), but every family is obligated to invite someone who does not have a family to celebrate the Passover with. Before every Passover Seder starts, the head of the household is to announce, *"Let all who are hungry come and eat with us!"* If only the poor and hungry of our communities would know that this invitation has been extended this night, how we would be blessed!

> **"If you extend your soul to the hungry and satisfy the afflicted soul, then your light shall dawn in the darkness..."** (Is. 58:10)

Preparing for the Seder

Every synagogue usually has a committee to link up those who are alone with a family for Pesach. My mother taught us the importance of this mitzvah (good deed), by always scanning the synagogues for some lost or lonely soul to invite to our feast tables. The Word says God sets the solitary in families (Ps. 68:6). We are commanded to practice gracious hospitality and to entertain strangers, some of whom might even be angels (Heb. 13:2). We are especially commanded to practice kindness to the strangers in the Land[1]. Perhaps there is someone new to the community or a foreigner to the country who would love to be invited to your Seder? We are exhorted, not to invite the rich and popular to our banqueting tables, but the poor, the maimed, the lost and lonely; those who can never pay us back. One year, in our congregation in Jerusalem, I had my eye on one elderly gentleman who always came in alone and usually left early without speaking to anyone. When the congregational leader asked who had nowhere to attend a Passover Seder, this man shyly put his finger up. It was with joy, then, that I invited him to our Seder and he accepted.

The day of the Seder, I must confess I was a total wreck. (Do we all have those days?). I felt as if I was rolling on waves of nausea from morning sickness and my hormones were definitely getting the better of me. My house lay in shambles - laundry, toys, and dirty dishes strewn all over the apartment, owing to my 'condition' – (well anyways, that was my excuse). To make the situation worse, the woman who had promised to come in and help clean and cook for the day called at the last minute to cancel. My apartment was too small and didn't even have a sofa; all we had to eat on was a plastic picnic table and I didn't own even one set of matching dishes. I felt terrible and looked worse. But I knew that this one, lonely, man was coming for Passover, as well as our two volunteers from South Africa, who would be celebrating

---

1 This is the most listed commandment in Tanach (Old Testament) - 36 times!

Passover with us in the Land for the very first time and I wanted it to be special for them. And so I got down on my knees and prayed, *"Oh Lord, you know how I feel and the circumstances in this home. I feel sorry for these people who are coming to our place for Passover, Lord, but please – do a miracle and somehow cause them to be blessed by sharing the Passover with us at our table."*

Incredibly – you probably can guess the end of the story – the house was cleaned, the table set, the food prepared, all by His grace. But the most wonderful blessing came through this elderly man, a Believer whose wife had died in childbirth along with their child. He had lived alone afterwards in Jerusalem for forty two years, keeping to himself, depending on the Lord for his daily bread, and so he had no one to celebrate Passover with. He sat with his face beaming, exclaiming throughout the Seder, "*What a blessing to be here! What a blessing*!" He even found an old missionary friend that he knew from long ago, who happened to live one block away from us and went to visit him. And so he said that the evening was not just a blessing, but a 'double blessing'! Please take courage from this story and reach out with your Passover Seder. You don't have to be perfect; you don't have to have a big house or nice furniture; you don't even have to know exactly how to hold a Seder; you just have to have a willing heart and say, *"Hineini Adonai"* (Here I am, Lord…)

The Seder Plate

The featured item on the Passover table is the Seder plate. This may be a specially purchased plate, of either glass or metal, with special designations for each item on the plate; or one can simply use a large serving platter and arrange the items in little bowls.

Elements of the Seder Plate

The following are the various elements placed on the Seder plate for use and explanation during the Seder:

1. Marror (bitter herbs) – either white or red horseradish may be used, fresh or from the jar. Warning: the fresh, white horseradish, ground just before the seder as my father used to do is extremely potent! It seemed to be used as some kind of 'macho initiation ceremony' for the new son-in-laws to have to endure a hefty helping of my Dad's horseradish on their matzah at their first family Passover (not recommended). The bitter herbs are to remind us of the bitterness of the Israelites' experience of slavery in Egypt. Custom holds that we have not really fulfilled the mitzvah (command) unless the portion we eat has brought tears to our eyes, as the slavery did to the Israelites. The children around my parent's table seemed to delight in watching the adults' faces turn red when they ate their portion of marror on matzah. Meanwhile, the kids secretly spit theirs out in napkins. Better to have LOTS of WATER on the table to drink after eating the marror. A small portion is placed on the seder plate for display and the rest in bowls placed on the table. Either the head of the table can pass around the matzah with marror, or each one can help themselves.

2. Charoset – a mixture of grated apples, crushed walnuts, sugar, cinnamon, and sweet, kiddush wine (to taste). Should somewhat resemble the brown, grainy, mortar used to make the bricks which the Israelites were forced to use in building the Egyptian pyramids (should resemble bricks in texture but not taste). The charoset may be displayed both as a small mound on the plate and a generous serving in a bowl for guests   The marror and charoset is often mixed together on the same piece of matzah as a kind of 'sandwich' to represent the bitter-sweet experience of life.

3. Carpas (Parsley) – greens represent spring and new life – the new life we have in Messiah. The parsley also represents the hyssop which was dipped in the blood of the Passover lamb and applied to the doors of the Israelites' homes.

4. Bowl of salt water – although not usually designated on the Seder plate, a bowl of salt water is necessary nearby to dip the greens into, representing the tears of life, and the tears of the Israelite slaves.

5. Roasted Egg – the origin and meaning of the roasted egg is a little dicey. Some believe it represents the cycle of life; others the mourning associated with the destruction of the temple. Still others believe its origin to correspond with pagan fertility rites, brought in from Babylon and therefore choose to omit the egg. Your call – your choice. For those who do include the egg, usually have one for display on the plate and a bowl of hard-boiled, peeled, cut in half eggs to also dip in the salt water.

6. Zroah (Shank bone) – this is the bone from the lamb, which of course must not be broken. Hopefully, it can be the bone from the lamb you have prepared and cooked for Passover. But many families substitute a large turkey bone. Lamb is of course better, but not always available. If turkey is used, it still must be used as if representing the sacrifice of the Passover Lamb. Some have asked me if we actually choose a lamb and keep it four days and then kill it on Passover and eat it. We do not do this for the reason that we believe Yeshua is the final sacrifice and therefore we do not need to perform the sacrifice of the lamb. We eat the lamb or at least hold up a bone and talk about it, to remember the sacrifice of Yeshua. The Passover lamb has not been sacrificed by the Jewish people since the destruction of the temple in 70 AD, although some sects of Samaritans (I believe) live in parts of Israel who do sacrifice the lamb.

Preparing for the Seder   111

7. *Hazzeret* – there is another place on the seder plate, which I have yet to learn exactly the difference between marror and hazzeret. Perhaps I will soon be enlightened. They both seem to represent bitter herbs. My mother used to put romaine lettuce in this spot. The six points on the Seder plate, therefore, (not including salt water) make up the shape of the Star of David.[2]

Other Elements on the Seder Table:

Not included on the Seder plate itself, but finding a place on the table (besides all the plates, cutlery, cups, wine glasses, and napkins) are the following items:

1. *Matzah* (unleavened bread): Usually three pieces of matzah are placed in a special tri-part cloth holder called a matzah tash. These are usually beautifully decorated for Pesach in either hand painted silk or embroidery. But one need not get caught up in having to be fancy. Three matzot (plural for matzah) placed on a tray on the table will do fine. The origin of this custom of the three matzot is not clear, but Messianics would claim that this is an ancient tradition originating in Messianic Passover Seders held by the early apostles, with the three matzot representing the Father, the Son and the Holy Spirit. When we proceed with the explanation of the Seder, you will see how clearly the matzah represents the Messiah. Another tray (special matzah trays are available which hold a stack of matzot nicely in place), should be placed on the table for general eating, whereas the three matzot are for ritual purposes.

---

[2] Some object to the use of the six-pointed Star of David as a symbol, owing to its questionable origins. Some claim that it is an occultic or mystical symbol, while others claim it was a gift given King David by one of his wives. Whatever the origin, it has become a universal symbol for Israel and Judaism. Whether or not to use it, is again a matter of personal conscience, through the guidance of the Holy Spirit.

2. *White linen cloth* – should be available to wrap the half of the middle matzah during the seder.

3. *Bowl of water* – for washing of hands (or feet?), hand towel on hand to dry fingers is helpful to have one less time to jump up from the table.

Note: make sure you don't mix up the vegetable dipping water with the hand washing water! We use a sprig of we parsley to designate the dipping bowl and a slice of lemon to indicate the finger dipping bowl.

4. *Wine* and grape juice – since four cups of wine are poured during the meal, it's best to have enough on hand and some grape juice for kids or abstainers. Usually special sweet, red, Kiddush wine is used such as Magen David or Carmel. At least use red to represent the blood of the New Covenant, and not white wine. This is not a social drinking event, but a serious religious ritual, which Yeshua commanded us to observe. Note: for all those silently screaming right now about the use of wine in a Passover Seder, may I remind you that Yeshua did not change the water into grape juice at the wedding in Cana. Wine has long been used in Jewish religious ceremonies, and represents the joy of the Spirit (new wine). Although we are not to get drunk, the Bible does not forbid the drinking of wine or alcoholic drink in moderation (See Deut. 14:26). Drinking wine is also not a requirement, so those who have a problem with this, can freely drink grape juice, as long as we don't judge one another for partaking of those things that are fully permissible in scripture. One of the ironies of some denominations of Christianity is the prohibition against things permissible in scripture (dance, wine, etc) and the license to indulge in things that are forbidden (eating of flesh of swine, shellfish, etc).

Preparing for the Seder

5. *The table* - Candles, matches, candle holder, a white tablecloth (special clear, thin, plastic sheets can be purchased to cover your beautiful, white holiday tablecloths and protect them from all the invariable spills during the Seder.

6. *Cup of Elijah* – According to Jewish tradition, the prophet Eliyahu (Elijah) will come before the coming of the Messiah (Malachi 4:5). Therefore Jewish people set an extra place setting, including a cup of wine and chair for Elijah. This empty place setting represents the hope of redemption, of the soon coming Messiah. A song is sung during the Seder about Eliyahu Hanavi (Elijah the prophet) who will come with Mashiach ben David (Messiah son of David). At one point in the Seder, someone (usually a child) opens the door to check and see if Elijah has perhaps come this year, heralding the arrival of the long awaited Messiah. Some Messianics object to observing this custom, since they believe John the Baptist (Yochanan the Immerser) already fulfilled this role in preparing the way for Yeshua, and that when the Messiah returns, He will come in the clouds and every eye will see Him. Again, this is your call by the guidance of the Holy Spirit.

CHAPTER FOURTEEN

ORDER OF THE SEDER

All right, the preparations are complete, the guests are assembled around your table, how does one proceed with the Seder?[1] The following will hopefully serve as a guide:

1. Light the festive candles
2. *Kiddush* – the first cup of wine (sanctification)
3. *Urchatz* – the washing of hands
4. *Carpas* – parsley dipped in salt water
5. *Matzah* – the blessing of the matzah
6. *Yachatz* – breaking the middle matzah and hiding half
7. *Marror* – eating of the bitter herbs
8. *Charoset* – eating of the apple/nut mixture
9. *Mah nishtanah* – the youngest child asks the four questions
10. *Magid* – tell the story of Passover
11. *Eser Makot* – the Ten plagues – the second cup of wine
12. *Pesach* – the lamb
13. *Shulchan Orech* – the festive meal
14. *Afikomen* – and third cup of redemption
15. *Hallel* – praise and the fourth cup
16. Next year in Jerusalem!

---

[1] *Note:* It is usually the husband and father who leads the Passover Seder as the head of the house. If there is no husband or father present, then the one acting as the head of the house in his absence may lead or a designated leader may be chosen.

Order of the Seder

1. We Light the Candles

The seder begins with the woman of the house if possible, lighting the festival candles with a blessing. Since the traditional Jewish blessings states that we are sanctified by the commandments and commanded to light the candles (which we are not, Biblically speaking), most Messianics adapt this blessing to something of the following form:

> "Baruch atah adonai, eloheinu melekh ha'olam, asher kidshanu b'dam Yeshua, Uvishmo anachnu madlikim neirot shel yom tov."

> "Blessed are you, O Lord our God, king of the Universe, who has sanctified us by the blood of Yeshua and in His name we light the festival candles."

I believe we are free to pray from our hearts, and the woman may express her heart in dedicating the Passover Seder, blessing all who attend, asking for the illumination of the Light of the World into this Seder. As the woman kindles the festival lights, we may pause to remember that it was through a Jewish maiden named Miryam that the Redeemer, the Light, came into this world.

2. The First Cup of Wine: (Kiddush)
The Cup of Sanctification

Four cups of wine are served throughout the Seder meal, representing the four promises God gave to the children of Israel (Ex. 6:6-7).

..........**I will bring you out from under the yoke of the Egyptians**
..........**I will free (rescue) you from being slaves**
..........**I will redeem you with an outstretched arm**
..........**I will take you as my own people, and I will be your God**

Those in the Land of Israel often add a fifth cup of wine in remembrance of the fifth promise:

..........**And I will bring you into the Land which I swore to give to Abraham, Isaac, and Jacob; and "I will give it to you as a heritage; I am YHVH (יהוה)"** (Ex. 6:8)

The Kiddush comes from the root, kadesh, which means 'holy, set apart, or sanctified. The first cup of sanctification reminds us that we are a holy nation, a royal priesthood, made up of Jews and Gentiles who have been set apart and sealed by the Holy Spirit for the purpose of serving the Holy One of Israel.

We lift up our first cup together and bless the Lord with the traditional blessing over wine:

> "Baruch atah adonai, eloheinu melech ha'olam, borei pri hagafen"

> "Blessed are you Lord, our God, King of the Universe, who creates the fruit of the vine."

We all drink the first cup of Passover

3. Urchatz - We Wash

Rather than seeing this custom as a fulfillment of the tradition of the elders regarding the ritual washing of hands before meals, we may see the example of humility and service that Yeshua set for us in the washing of His disciples; feet.

> **"Now that I, your Lord and Teacher, have washed your feet, you also should wash one another's feet."** (John 13:12-14)

Some prefer to actually wash one another's feet at the Passover, but for those who find their inhibitions getting in the way, a modified custom is to wash and dry one another's hands in the water bowl as an expression of love, service, and humility.

4. Karpas - Parsley

Lifting up both the parsley and the salt water, the leader explains how life, represented by the greens, sometimes comes with tears. We are reminded of the tears of the Israelite slaves in Egypt; perhaps we could also remember the tears of all the Israelites today who weep with every terror attack in the Land of Israel. May we also remember that our hope is one day to live in that place where there will no longer be any tears or sorrow or death.

We recite the blessing together and then eat the parsley dipped in salt water:

> "Baruch atah adonai, eloheinu melech ha'olam borei pri ha'adamah."

"Blessed are you, Lord our God, King of the Universe who has created the fruit of the earth."

5. Matzah

The leader holds up a square (or round) of matzah and explains how we eat this unleavened bread to remember how the children of Israel fled from Egypt in such haste that they didn't even have time for their bread to rise. We also eat the unleavened bread to remember that we are to strive to be without leaven (sin) in our lives. Let us pray to break old sinful habits and live a new life of holiness.

Eating the Bread of Affliction

The matzah is also known as the 'bread of affliction'. The Messiah, who was the sinless lamb (without any leaven), was well acquainted with grief and sorrow.

The more the Egyptians oppressed the Israelites, the more they grew and multiplied. Usually, we fear and hate oppression and affliction for the pain and suffering it brings us. But it is often in these hard places that we grow spiritually. During Passover we eat unleavened bread, also called the 'bread of affliction'. If we do not eat this dry, hard, tasteless bread, during the season of Passover, we will be 'cut off from our people.' Are we willing to eat the 'bread of affliction' if God chooses to place us under the yoke of oppression for a season in order to grow and mature? We must trust that God is in control, even during the painful experiences of our lives, and that He is working in us to perfect us into the image of His son, who was well acquainted with grief and sorrows. In all our afflictions, He is also afflicted. We must not lose heart, for we will reap an abundant harvest and walk out 'with a high hand' also, if we persevere.

The matzah also represents the Messiah in its symbolism in that it is striped and pierced. The Messiah was

> **"Wounded for our transgressions, he was bruised for our iniquities; the chastisement of our peace was upon him; and <u>with his stripes</u> we are healed."**
> (Is. 53:5)

We are also reminded of the words of the Hebrew prophet that one day, the inhabitants of Jerusalem will look upon Him (the Messiah) <u>whom they have pierced</u>, and will recognize him and mourn for Him as one mourns for an only son. (Zech. 12:10)

6. Yachatz

Yachatz is the breaking of the middle matzah from the three special matzot contained in the matzah holder (tash). That these three matzot may represent the Father, the Son and the Holy Spirit. The middle matzah, therefore, represents the 'Son'. The leader holds up this matzah and breaks it in half, then wraps the broken piece in a white linen cloth or napkin. This special piece, now called the afikomen, is then hidden away by the leader in a secret place while the children close their eyes. After the Seder meal, the children will search for the afikomen and bring it out again. The leader must pay the 'ransom' demanded by the children to receive the afikomen back in order to continue the Seder. The leader can explain the symbolism of this ritual – the broken matzah represents the broken body of Messiah, which was wrapped in white burial cloth, hidden away in the tomb for three days and three nights and then resurrected to new life.

It is amazing when we consider that the same ritual is practiced in every traditional Jewish Seder, and yet without the revelation of the death, burial and resurrection of the Messiah.

Holding the unwrapped half of the matzah, the leader can

recite the blessing over the matzah and all may share a piece of the unleavened bread of Passover.

> "Baruch atah adonai, Eloheinu melech ha'olam, hamotzi lechem min ha'aretz."
>
> "Blessed are you Lord our God, King of the Universe, who brings forth bread out of the earth."

7. Marror - The Bitter Herbs

The bitter herbs represent the bitterness of the life of slavery that the Israelites experienced in Egypt.

> **"...so the Egyptians came to dread the Israelites and worked them ruthlessly. They made their lives bitter with hard labor in brick and mortar and with all kinds of work in the fields."** (Ex. 1:13-14)

We may also remember all those who suffer in the bitterness of spiritual bondage all around us – praying that they may be set free this Passover. Even as the Israelites could not listen at first to Moses, because they were so bitter, let us not be discouraged when people reject our message that God has sent a Redeemer to set them free. The leader scoops some horseradish onto a piece of matzah and recites the blessing, asking that we would remember with compassion the sorrow of our ancestors in Egypt long ago, but also the grief of the people of Israel today.

> "Baruch atah adonai eloheinu melech ha'olam asher kidshanu b'dvaro v'tzivanu al achilat marror."

"Blessed are You, Lord our God, King of the Universe, who has set us apart by His word and commanded us to eat bitter herbs."

All may eat a portion of bitter herbs (horseradish) on a piece of matzah.

8. Charoset

The leader scoops a teaspoon of the sweet, apple/nut mixture onto a piece of matzah and explains how this represents the brick and clay mortar which the Israelites labored with to build the Egyptian cities for Pharaoh. The charoset is then dipped into the marror and eaten together on a piece of matzah. This reminds us that sometimes life experiences are bitter but they can be sweetened by the hope we have in God. Eating the marror and charoset together represents the 'bitter-sweet' experience of life. All may eat of this 'sandwich'.

9. Mah Nishtanah - Why is this night different than all other night?

(The Four Questions)

Our children are encouraged to ask questions throughout the Seder. In a formal way, this is represented by the asking of the four questions (mah nishtanah?), which means 'what is changed?' Usually the youngest child (just 'cause they're so cute when they sing!) stands up and chants the mah nishtanah. In Israel, we have the advantage that our children are taught this song in every school. Jewish children are also taught this traditional melody in Hebrew schools. But for others, Passover tapes are available (both traditional and Messianic) which contain the words and the tunes for the traditional Passover songs. If you can't find a tape, just improvise – have the children make up their own questions about Passover to ask (and you'd better have answers ready!).

Note: There is usually a limited time span during which any child is both competent and comfortable in standing up in front of a whole group of people and singing four questions. This varies, but lies somewhere between the ages of four and fourteen (although our two-year old boldly chimes in). A nice idea is to have a group of children sing together (get out those video cameras for that special moment). Don't do as was done to me and embarrass a teenager by forcing them to sing the four questions in their adolescent self-conscious state. I ended up locking myself for the whole Passover Seder in our bathroom) when I, at the age of 15, happened to be the youngest at the table!

The four questions the children ask are these:

1. *Why* is it that on every other night we eat bread and tonight we eat only matzah?
2. *Why* is it that on every other night we eat other vegetables and tonight we eat only bitter herb?
3. *Why* is it that on every other night, we don't even dip our vegetables once but tonight we dip twice?
4. *Why* is it that on every other night, we have to sit straight at the table but tonight we can recline?

10. Magid – Tell the Story of Passover

Here we come to the 'meat' of the Seder – the Passover narration. There is no right or wrong way to do this. Some might want to take turns around the table with readings from Exodus chapter 12. Others may find more creative ways to re-tell the story. Children are great at making this fun! When our daughter, Liat, was two years old, she played the part of Miriam, sister of baby Moses, using a cheapo baby doll in a wicker basket we found at a toy store. Her then eight-year-old brother played the part of the 'bad guys' – the Egyptians who were trying to find all the Hebrew babies to throw them into the Nile. This impromptu play was made easier by the fact that the children had watched the Prince of Egypt video seemingly hundreds of times! (Good videos are limited in Israel)

I, of course, played the part of baby Moses' mother. We hid the baby doll in our cloak, ran down to the 'river' (under the dining table), held baby Moses and prayed that God would keep him safe, cried a little, and then put him in his basket and sent him on down the river (throwing in some plastic fish for effects). This play went on and on, with spontaneous improvisations, making up the script as we went along. We used a baby stuffed lamb, which my son killed with his toy sword, to put its blood on our door. Sometimes it helps to act these things out in order to really grasp the reality of what was happening to the Israelites – to feel their emotions, rather than just read it as a story. What struck me when we dramatized the Passover story was how frightened the children must have been. Liat and I sat huddled together inside our house while outside; the angel of death visited each home and killed the firstborn of every Egyptian. My son was making a great, dramatic display of this with a black cloak, and Liat cried out, *"Mommy, I'm scared!"*. I instinctively replied, *"It's all right, don't be scared; the blood of the lamb is on our door."* I kept repeating, *"the blood of the lamb, the blood of the lamb"*, to reassure the child. What a comfort to know that wherever we are and in whatever frightening situation we find ourselves, we need not fear because the blood of the lamb is covering us and God will not permit the destroyer to enter!

No Seder is complete without songs and some favorites of the children to sing at this time are 'Go down Moses' and 'Avadim Hayinu' (Once we were slaves). Try to find a good Passover tape or Bible sing along for children with these songs.

11. The Second Cup of Wine: (Eser Makot) The Ten Plagues

When we come to the point in the story describing the ten plagues, we stop to pour the second cup of wine. God sent plagues upon Egypt, and yet with each one, Pharaoh hardened his heart and refused to let Israel go. When we recall the pouring out of God's judgment upon Egypt in the form of the ten plagues, the issue of covenant becomes exceedingly precious to us. The scriptures show that God made a clear distinction between those who were 'His' and those who dwelt outside the place of covenant. While flies swarmed all over Egypt, no swarms of flies plagued Goshen, where the Israelites dwelled.

> **"And in that day I will set apart the land of Goshen, in which My people dwell, that no swarms of flies shall be there, in order that you may know that I am the Lord in the midst of the land. I will make a difference between My people and your people."**
> (Ex. 8:22-23)

It was and still is not a matter of favoritism, but of covenant.

The people of Israel were set apart, sanctified, made into a holy nation by God's election and grace and because He loved their forefathers and made unbreakable promises to them. He has done the same for every man, woman and child in covenant with Him through the blood of the Messiah, Yeshua. We can claim the protection of the blood, even in the midst of any plagues which are being poured out all around us.

> "A thousand may fall at your side, and ten thousand at your right hand; but it shall not come near you. Only with your eyes shall you look, and see the reward of the wicked. Because you have made the Lord, who is my refuge, even the Most High, your dwelling place, no evil shall befall you, nor shall any plague come near your dwelling."
> (Ps. 91:7-10)

I don't believe we will be taken out of this earth when God's judgment once again falls, but this time upon the whole earth – all the nations – specifically for coming against Israel and Jerusalem. But the example of the Exodus shows us that God is well able to protect His people, even in the midst of His plagues. We can take comfort in this and find rest in Him, despite the increasingly chaotic state of world events as the return of the Redeemer draws near.

The offer of a place in the covenant of promise is not restricted to the Jewish people now but open to anyone of any tongue, tribe or nationality – including the Egyptians and the other Arabic peoples. Whoever feared the word of the Lord among the servants of Pharaoh made his servants and his livestock flee to the houses.

> "But he who did not regard the word of the Lord left his servants and his livestock in the field."
> (Ex. 9:21)

And they suffered.

> "Only in the land of Goshen, where the children of Israel were, there was no hail." (Ex. 9:26)

Only those who have truly taken shelter under the wings of

the God of Israel will be safe in the coming times. Those who are against Israel are against the Lord and outside His covenant of promise, no matter what label or denomination they consider themselves!

These plagues were not random, but represented God's supremacy over all the false gods of Egypt.

> **"On that same night I will pass through Egypt and strike down every firstborn – both men and animals – and I will bring judgment on all the gods of Egypt;"** (Ex. 12:12)

Many people believe they are praying to God, but they may actually be following a false god, as were the Egyptians. When I was searching for God in New Age religion and philosophies, I considered the 'cosmic consciousness' or generic 'higher power' to be my God. But there is only one true God, Elohim, YHVH {יהוה}, the God of my Fathers, Abraham, Isaac, and Jacob; whereas, there are many false gods. The Passover story helped me to see this truth and break out of the deception of New Age. The plague of darkness demonstrated God's power of the supreme Egyptian god, Ra, the sun god. With the final plague, the death of the firstborn, Pharaoh finally relented. Because Egypt refused to let Israel, God's firstborn, go, God pronounced judgment on all the firstborn of the Egyptians. This is another example that what any individual or nation does to Israel, whether for good or for evil, will return back upon them.

As You Do To Others

The King of Egypt decreed that all male Hebrew babies would be drowned in the Nile River. In the end, however, we see that the male Egyptians in Pharaoh's army were all drowned in the Sea of Reeds. God has promised that He will put the curses back upon the heads of those who hate Israel. He promised Abraham and his seed, "I will bless those who bless you and curse those who curse you." (Gen. 12:3) What one endeavors to do towards Israel will come back upon them, whether for good or for evil. Haman, in the Book of Esther, who tried to annihilate all the Jews, was hung on the very gallows that he built to hang Mordechai the Jew. God has declared Israel to be the 'apple of His eye'. (Zech.2:8) Whoever attempts to harm her is, in effect, poking their finger in the pupil of God's eye. I certainly would not want to be that person. God has an issue with the nations of the earth for how they have treated His people while they wandered in exile from country to country – the wandering Jews. In almost every nation, even up to modern times, the Jews have been exiled, persecuted, and slaughtered. In many instances, those who called themselves Christians led the slaughter in the 'name of Christ' and under the symbol of the cross. Is it any wonder that Jewish people do not want to 'convert' to be Christians?

> **"For the day of the Lord upon all the nations is near; as you have done, it shall be done to you; Your reprisal shall return upon your own head."**
> (Obad. 1:15)

For each plague, the leader followed by all those participating in the Seder dip their little finger into the cup of wine and drop it onto their plate as they say the name of each plague (Hebrew is best, but English or any language will do!).

According to tradition, each plague is recited three times.

Blood! **Dum!**
Frogs!   **Tz'fardeyah!**
Lice! **Kinim!**
Beasts!   **Arov!**

Cattle Disease!	**Dever!**
Boils!	**Sh'chin!**
Hail!	**Barad!**
Locusts!	**Arbeh!**
Darkness!	**Hoshekh!**
Death of the Firstborn!	**Makat B'chorot!!**

Traditionally, many do not drink the second cup but pour it out and throw it away, in remembrance of God's word that we will not drink from His cup of wrath again, but that He will give the cup to our enemies.

> **"See, I have taken out of your hand**
> **the cup of poison,**
> **the dregs of the cup of My fury;**
> **you shall no longer drink it.**
> **But I will put it into the hand of**
> **those who afflict you..."** (Is. 51:22-23)

12. Pesach - The Lamb

At this point, the leader holds up the z'roah (shank bone), which represents the lamb whose blood marked the houses of the children of Israel for protection.

> **"The blood will be a sign for you on the houses where you are; and when I see the blood, I will pass over you."** (Ex. 12:13)

If one wants to make this even more real and interactive for the children, they can paint or color strips of red paper and paste them on the doorposts and lintels of their homes for Passover. If anyone asks about these, it would make an excellent discussion starter about the Passover Lamb and the protection found in its blood. We who are followers of Yeshua believe that He is the fulfillment of the Passover Lamb.

> **"Behold! The Lamb of God who takes away the sin of the world!"** (John 1:29)

In a vision that John describes in the book of Revelation, the Lion of the tribe of Judah, the Root of David (the Messiah), has prevailed to open the scroll and to loose its seven seals (the beginning of the final plagues). (Rev. 5:5). He then describes the lamb standing as though it had been slain. All the elders fall down before the lamb and sing,

> **"Worthy is the Lamb who was slain to receive power and riches and wisdom, and strength and honor and glory and blessing."** (Rev. 5:13)

Songs of praise and worship are sung to the One who sits on the throne and unto the LAMB. As the plagues fall upon the earth, men still refuse to humble themselves and repent, just as Pharaoh stayed hard in his heart towards God. In fear, they seek to hide from the face of Him who sits on the throne and from the **'...wrath of the Lamb.'** (Rev. 6:16)

Yes, the lamb of God is not only to be remembered from the past, but is very much a part of our lives today and will play a significant role in the future of the fate of mankind.

Note: This is a highly appropriate place, especially in a congregational setting, to pray a prayer of salvation for anyone who is not certain that they are covered by the blood of the Passover Lamb of God, Yeshua the Messiah. It is also time for those who have left the covering of His blood to 'walk the streets of Egypt' to make a commitment to return to a set-apart life of holiness and re-dedication to God.

This is also a wonderful time to sing special songs such as 'Lamb of God' or in Hebrew, 'Seh Ha'elohim'.

13. Shulchan Orech – The Festive Meal

By now most people are hungry and ready for a delicious festive meal. Any Jewish cookbook will give many traditional Passover recipes using matzah meal and unleavened products. A standard appetizer is gefilte fish on a bed of lettuce and served with tomatoes, cucumbers and sliced onion. This is often followed by special matzah ball chicken soup, which is often available as a mix for those of us used to Western convenience cooking. Usually a roast chicken, turkey, or roast beef is served, or lamb along with vegetable side dishes and special Passover desserts (brownies are a favorite). The egg for those who do use the roasted egg as a symbol of mourning over the destruction of the second temple may be eaten during the Seder meal.

14. The Third Cup of Redemption and the Afikomen

After the meal, when the children start to get restless, they may begin searching for the afikomen. This can also be done in a congregation, but be ready to have a prize for the one who finds it. The leader or head of the table must ransom this piece of matzah back in order to carry on the Seder. We are reminded that the Son of man came to serve us and to give His life a ransom for many. (Matt. 20:28). The leader may remind us that the afikomen represents the broken body of the Son of God, Yeshua, which has been hidden away, but now has been raised up again. Yeshua said,

> **"I am the resurrection and the life. He who believes in Me, though he may die, he shall live."**
> (John 11:25)

The resurrection is not just an afterthought, but central to our faith. In fact, without the hope of the resurrection, our faith is empty and meaningless.

> **"But if there is no resurrection of the dead, then Messiah is not risen. And if Messiah is not risen, then our preaching is empty and your faith is also empty."** (1 Cor. 15:13-14)

Resurrection is not just a 'Christian' or New Testament concept as many Jewish people consider. Our own prophet, Daniel, spoke of a resurrection of the dead and judgment.

> **"Multitudes who sleep in the dust of the earth will awake: some to everlasting life, others to shame and everlasting contempt."** (Dan. 12:2)

In The Belly of the Whale

Yeshua promised that, just as Jonah was in the belly of the whale for three days and three nights, so would He remain three days and three nights in the heart of the earth. (Matt. 12:39-40). He gave this as a sign that He is who He claims to be; therefore if His words did not come true with one hundred percent accuracy, He could not be considered a true prophet. Believing in a Friday crucifixion and an Easter Sunday resurrection casts doubt on Yeshua's authenticity since this does not account for three days and three nights in the grave. The confusion arises over the fact that they had to get the body of Yeshua off the cross before the 'Sabbath'. Many consider this a regular seventh day Sabbath, but in fact, it was a 'High Sabbath', as the first day of the Feast is considered. (John 19:31) This High Sabbath may occur on any day of the week. (Lev. 23:7). When was Yeshua resurrected? We know that it occurred sometime before dawn on Sunday morning because when the women came to check His body, after resting on the seventh day Sabbath as commanded, He was already gone from the tomb. (Matt. 28:1,6) Sunday, according to Jewish tradition, the first day of the week, begins at sunset or dusk on Saturday evening, called Motzei Shabbat. I believe that Yeshua was raised on Motzei Shabbat and that if we count back three days and three nights, we come to a Wednesday at dusk crucifixion, which lines up with the 14th of Nissan for that year. Now, before I get a whole flood of letters taking up controversy with what I've just written, let me remind you that this is only my view and that I do not profess to be any type of scholar, simply a student of the Bible as we all are. And it's an open book for all.

The most important point to keep in mind, rather than getting bogged down in dates and times, is the fact that Yeshua was raised from the dead as the "firstfruits" or bikkurim in Hebrew, of all who will be raised from death to life after Him.

> **"But now Messiah is risen from the dead, and has become the firstfruits of those who have fallen asleep… For as in Adam all die, even so in Messiah all shall be made alive. But each one in his own order; Messiah the firstfruits, afterward those who are Messiah's at His coming."** (1 Cor. 15:20, 22-23)

The Matzah and the Cup

After reminding us of the resurrection, symbolized by the afikomen, the leader raises this special piece of matzah and repeats Yeshua's words at His last Passover Seder,

> **"This is my body given for you; do this in remembrance of me."** (Luke 22:19)

As the leader breaks the pieces of afikomen and passes them

around to everyone at the Seder, we eat our portion in remembrance of all that Yeshua has done for us, as He asked us to do each Passover. We also hold up the third cup, the Cup of Redemption, and repeat Yeshua's words over this same cup,

> **"This cup is the new covenant in my blood, which is poured out for you."** (Luke 22:20)

What is this new covenant Yeshua spoke of? It is the covenant God promised to the House of Judah and the House of Israel through the prophet Jeremiah, an everlasting covenant of peace and forgiveness of sins, of a new and living relationship with our God.

The New Covenant

> **"Behold, the days are coming, says the Lord, when I will make a new covenant with the House of Israel and with the House of Judah – not according to the covenant that I made with their fathers in the day that I took them by the hand to lead them out of the land of Egypt, My covenant which they broke, though I was a husband to them, says the Lord. But this is the covenant that I will make with the house of Israel after those days, says the Lord; I will put My law (Torah) in their minds, and write it on their hearts; and I will be their God, and they shall be My people…For I will forgive their iniquity and their sin I will remember no more."** (Jer. 31:31-34)

What a wonderful promise to Israel! And the good news is that it is not limited to Israel, for the Messiah's role was to bring salvation to all of mankind! Halleluyah! There was only one problem with this promised new covenant. At this time, it had not yet been sealed in blood; and all covenants must be sealed in blood. (Heb. 9:18-22). This is the most awesome thing that Yeshua accomplished, which we remember with this cup – He sealed this eternal covenant bringing peace between us and God with His own blood.

> **"Not with the blood of goats and calves, but with His own blood He entered the Most holy Place once for all, having obtained eternal redemption."**
> (Heb. 9:12)

As we drink this third cup of redemption, we remember our Savior, Yeshua, who sealed the new covenant in His blood. All drink.

Note: If you hadn't noticed, this is the actual 'communion service' in its Hebraic context that Yeshua intended. I don't believe that 'communion' was ever meant to be a regular 'Sunday event', but that when we celebrate our Passover Seder and come to this point, we are to always remember Yeshua. The Catholic Church perverted this remembrance of Yeshua at Passover into a weekly Sunday morning observance. Pagans were already holding a Sunday service to worship the sun deity, and used a flat disc of bread. The moment the Pagan priest would lift it into the air to receive the sun's rays, it became transformed or 'transubstantiated' into the actual presence of the sun. They believed that by eating it, they would possess the powers of the deity. Although we now use the words 'abracadabra and hocus pocus' as superstitious or silly magical nonsense, Pagans took these words very seriously to transform the 'wafer' into the power of the sun god. These ceremonies obviously were an abomination to God. The 'Last Supper' was not a 'mass' but a regular Passover Seder, which the Jewish people had celebrated year after year for centuries. Although it is not our position to judge our brothers and sisters, it is vital that we become enlightened about this information for the sake of our own spiritual health and the authenticity of our relationship with the one, true Elohim, יהוה (YHVH).

This doesn't mean it is a sin to do it more often, only that I don't believe it was Yeshua's original intention. The cup is never to be served with bread containing yeast as some churches do. As you may probably discern by this point, people who do this are symbolically ingesting their sins. The Word warns us to never offer up the cup of sacrifice along with leavened bread. (Ex. 23:18) This is just one of the side effects of the divorce between the Church and their Jewish roots. The children of the divorce no longer recognize their heritage. But God is doing a wonderful work by His Spirit and celebrating the Passover is one way of re-connecting and healing the split.

15. The Fourth Cup and Hallel (Praise)

As we sit in awe and gratitude in renewed awareness of all that Yeshua has done for us, we may collectively sing or recite psalms of praise and songs of worship to the Lord.

This is the last cup of wine, the cup of praise, which Yeshua said He would drink with us in the Kingdom, at the marriage supper of the Lamb. I hope to see you ALL there!

16. Next Year in Jerusalem!

The Passover Seder ends with the joyful shout, "L'shana Haba'ah B'Yirushalayim" (Next Year in Jerusalem!!) The Jerusalem of today exists as a far cry from the Holy City that God intended. Anyone who has lived there would probably admit (if they are honest) that it is full of sin and uncleanness. Jerusalem reached a new low with the approval of a gay parade for the 'holy city'. Scripture calls Jerusalem spiritually Sodom and Egypt. (Rev.

11:8) Sadly, this is true. This Jerusalem is in the flesh, which is in bondage with her children. (Gal. 4:25) Many of us long to celebrate and even live in Jerusalem, but it is actually a longing for the 'New Jerusalem' which God has placed in our hearts. **"but the Jerusalem above is free, which is the mother of us all."** (Gal. 4:26) The city of God to which we all aspire and hope for is the New Jerusalem which will come down from heaven.

> **"I will write on him the name of My God and the name of the city of My God, the New Jerusalem, which comes down out of heaven from My God. "**
> (Rev. 3:12)

This city will be filled with joy, peace, and righteousness. (Isa. 65:18) She will be the praise of the whole earth. (Isa. 62:7) One day we will all be comforted in this Jerusalem. (Isa. 66:13) Too many people confuse the two, expecting the Jerusalem of the modern state of Israel to be holy. It cannot be until the day Yeshua comes and the people receive Him. Therefore, as we give this joyful shout to the Lord, let us say, "L'shana ha'ba'ah b'Yirushalayim Hahadashah!" (Next year in the New Jerusalem!)

CHAPTER FIFTEEN

WHAT ABOUT EASTER?

Well, our Passover Seder is complete. We have eaten the matzah, the marror and the lamb; we have narrated the story of our exodus from Egypt, explained the significance of our redemption in Yeshua, the Passover lamb, remembered his death by crucifixion with the cup and matzah; re-enacted his burial and resurrection with the afikomen. There is only one nagging question left to deal with – what about Easter?

Once again, I almost hate to disturb our satisfied, wine and food overstuffed complacency by bringing up a contentious point, but it seems that the issue need to be addressed. Even as a Jewish girl, I realize that Easter is a well-established and for the most part beloved Christian tradition. It represents to many people all over the world, one of the most important aspects of our faith – the resurrection of the Messiah from death to life. In fact, Paul says if we don't believe the resurrection happened, then our faith is null and void or pointless. I also enjoyed, in my early years as a Believer, participating in the Easter plays, singing, *"He's alive again!"* from my position in the choir. Easter, however, is not a Biblically commanded festival; it also contains elements of pagan worship of a fertility goddess named Ischtar. This information is not meant to be presented as a judgment upon those who do celebrate Easter, but only as information for consideration.

The Development of Easter

Easter (Ostara, or Eastre) was the name of the goddess of Spring and fertility in the religion of the ancient Anglo-Saxons. They held a celebration in her honor every April. Long before Christianity came along, pagans (those not in covenant with YHVH) observed Easter as one of their biggest celebrations. The Assyrians, the Phoenicians and the Philistines all celebrated Easter. The festival was instituted at the Spring Equinox when pagans believed that the sun impregnated the Earth Mother. Celebrants engaged in ritual sex acts and used symbols of fertility such as eggs, rabbits, and hot cross buns. These round cakes were baked for the 'Queen of Heaven' with the cross symbol, the Babylonian sign for the female. Pagans colored eggs in the bright colors of spring, hoping to insure a prosperous growing season, and then hid them from evil spirits in rabbits' dens – another symbol of fertility. 'Easter' is the name of the Babylonian fertility goddess, the Queen of Heaven, the 'mother of harlots described in Revelation 17. Her image stands as the 'Lady liberty' statue in the New York Harbor, complete with the tower headpiece as worn by Artemis, a false goddess. Her emblem is the lily flower, which most churches use to decorate for Easter.

How did the church come to be 'entangled' with pagan Easter rather than continue the observation of the Biblical Passover? Christianity's contamination with paganism began with one man specifically – the Roman Emperor Constantine I. In the year 325 CE, he convened a council (the Nicene Council) with 220 Gentile elders (Jewish Believers had already been ostracized from the 'church' by this time). Their purpose was to establish a unity of basic doctrine and religious practices. The result of this was the formation of the Roman Catholic Church (Catholic means 'universal'), which absorbed all the pagans of the empire into this 'one world religion'. Rather than try to change the behavior of

99% of the pagans for the sake of the 1% minority who practiced 'The Way', they decided instead to absorb the pagans' existing religious practices and festivals into the new universal religion. In order to accommodate their established custom of worshipping the sun god on sun-day, the seventh day Sabbath was abolished and Sunday instituted as the day of worship. There is no scriptural basis for a change of the Sabbath day from the seventh day to the first and the Catholic Church openly admits to their responsibility for this man-made change. Constantine's council also outlawed the Torah, fulfilling the prophecy of Daniel 7:25:

> **"He will speak against the Most High and oppress His saints and try to change the set times (moadim/ Biblical Feasts) and the law (Torah)."**

The prophet, Jeremiah, soundly condemned this idolatrous worship of the Queen of Heaven.

> **"Therefore do not pray for this people, nor lift up a cry or prayer for them, nor make intercession to Me; for I will not hear you. Do you not see what they do in the cities of Judah and in the streets of Jerusalem? The children gather wood, the fathers kindle the fires, and the women knead dough, to make cakes for the queen of heaven; and they pour out drink offerings to other gods, that they may provoke Me to anger. Do they provoke Me to anger?" says the Lord. "Do they not provoke themselves, to the shame of their own faces?"**
> (Jer. 7:16-19)

We Will Not Listen!

The thanks that Jeremiah received for speaking the truth about the sin of false worship was to be thrown down a well. I hope I don't meet a similar fate, but it is still my responsibility to share what is the truth by the Word of God. I know that some will listen, but many will stubbornly refuse. Such things also happened in Israel long ago, as recounted in Jeremiah 44:16-17:

> **"As for the word that you have spoken to us in the name of the Lord, we will not listen to you! But we will certainly do whatever has gone out of our own mouth, to burn incense to the Queen of Heaven and pour out drink offerings to her as we have done, we and our fathers, our kings and our princes, in the cities of Judah and in the streets of Jerusalem."**

It seems to me that many would mouth similar words today, *"We will not listen to you! We will surely celebrate our Easter as we like, as did our parents and pastors and fellow Christians in all the nations of the world."*

Tradition is a very powerful force; it can be used for good or for evil. If our traditions, whether they be Jewish or Christian, contradict the word of God, then we must be willing to surrender them and instead adopt new customs which conform themselves to the Bible.

If we continue to do something simply because it is entrenched in our family generational line, or because it is what the church teaches, then we cannot criticize or judge the Jewish people who do the same. Yeshua rebuked the Jewish religious leaders for holding onto their traditions that contradict the word of God. (Matt.15:3) Perhaps His rebuke might be directed towards some

What About Easter?

of the Christian religious leaders of this day?

Sometimes people follow traditions blindly. A story is told of a young mother who always served her new husband roast beef with both ends cut off. Puzzled, the husband asked his bride one day why she always chopped off part of the beef? She answered that it was because her mother had always done so, and so they let the matter rest. But one day, out of curiosity, the young woman asked her mother why she had taught her to chop the ends off the roast. *"Oh"*, her elderly mother replied sweetly, *"My dear, I had to do that because my roasting pan was so very small."*

Nor can we claim innocence because our husbands or wives approve of these wrong forms of worship. We will all stand alone before God one day in judgment. The women of Israel also attempted to claim a lack of responsibility through their husband's covering,

> **"And when we burned incense to the queen of heaven and poured out drink offerings to her, did we make cakes for her, to worship her, and pour out drink offerings to her without our husbands' permission?"** (Jer. 44:19)

A Festival to the Lord

I can hear the indignant rumblings, *"We are not worshipping the queen of heaven when we celebrate Easter; we are celebrating a festival to the Lord!"* We may look into the Word of God to see how God feels about us making up our own feasts and festivals:

When Moses took a little too long up on the mountain for the people's comfort zone, they began to get restless, and so Aaron placated them with a golden calf. Aaron, the great appeaser, then made a proclamation,

> **"Tomorrow is a feast to יהוה."** (Ex. 32:5)

Notice, Aaron did not say, 'Tomorrow we will indulge in idolatrous revelry", but we will celebrate a feast to יהוה. Just because we put a Christian label on the feast, it does not magically wipe out its pagan roots, nor does it obligate God to put His stamp of approval on it. He did not command the celebration of Easter; it was a man-made feast, originating in pagan, heathen worship of false gods, therefore God's people are forbidden to imitate.

Do Not Worship Me in 'Their' (Pagan) Ways

Messiah and His followers kept "Passover" (Lev.23:5) the "Feast of Unleavened Bread," (Lev.23: 6-8) and the "Feast of Firstfruits."(Lev.23: 9-14.) They did not in any way keep the pagan holiday Easter. The followers of the Messiah were forbidden to keep pagan customs or traditions decreed to be abominations by the God of Abraham, Isaac and Jacob throughout the Old Testament. (Deut.12:4-31) Easter sunrise service is an ancient pagan custom of worship to the sun god "Tammuz" which at the time of the vernal equinox, was returning into the northern hemisphere from its journey south. The vernal equinox is a time of year when the sun crosses the equator on its trek northward. To Pagan worshippers, it is time to celebrate the return of life and reproduction to animal and plant life. This is why Ishtar, or Easter, was chosen to be celebrated at this time of year.

Now I know, as well as you do, that myriads of precious people celebrate Easter. The day I wrote this, it happened to be Easter day in Jerusalem and many sincere Christians were flocking to a special sunrise service at the Garden tomb that is supposedly the burial place of Yeshua. Many celebrate Easter as the resurrection of Yeshua. Is it possible that all these people are in error? Well, in Jewish fashion, let me answer with another question. Do you, as a Christian, believe that all the sincere and pious Jewish people in the world; all the Rabbinic sages who have devoted their lives to religious study, and who still don't believe Yeshua is the Messiah are in error? I understand that the majority of sincere Christians who celebrate Easter do so with the best of intentions, but then again, I know of many 'New Age' people who practice transcendental meditation and astrology with all sincerity in their desire to be holy and spiritually close to 'God'. Therefore, sincerity is not an excuse for practicing false worship. Our only sure guide can be the Word of God. He has not left us in ignorance regarding His will in the matter of feasts and festivals. He outlines each and every one in His book and commands us to celebrate them in the manner described. The Messiah is revealed in all of these festivals and therefore everything we need to remember and celebrate about Yeshua is contained in these feasts. I am quite certain that the death and resurrection of His Son did not come as a big surprise to God, since God has known the end from the beginning. If we needed a festival to remember His resurrection (other than Bikkurim, the Feast of Firstfruits), I am sure that His Word would have included it.

I once heard an excellent preacher on Middle East Television exhorting the Church to obedience. He said, *"God cares for you and loves you deeply, but He doesn't need you to improve upon His commandments!"* How true. God has not given us the task of making up our own feasts and festivals in His name or on His behalf. He has already taken care of this and our only role is to comply in unquestioning obedience. One of the Kings of Israel also attempted to improve upon God's appointed times by making up his own 'festival to the Lord'.

You would think that Israel would have learned their lesson from the first golden calf fiasco, but here we have Jeroboam, King of Israel, making not one but two golden calves and mouthing

Aaron's words again,

> **"Here are your gods, O Israel, which brought you up from the land of Egypt."** (1 Kin. 12:28)

We can see clearly that Israel had left Egypt, but Egypt had not yet been purged from Israel. They still clung to these leftover pagan, idolatrous practices. The Church has been called out of idolatry, out of the ways of 'Babylon', in order to take a place of covenant in the commonwealth of Israel, but many still also cling to some die-hard heathen customs and practices.

Devised in His Own Heart

What came out of this idolatry? Naturally, an idolatrous, man-made festival with a holy veneer.

> **"Jeroboam ordained a feast on the fifteenth day of the eight month"** (1 Kin. 12:32)

Nowhere in His Word does God command such a feast. So where did Jeroboam get such an idea? He devised it in his own heart:

> **"So he made offerings on the altar which he had made at Bethel on the fifteenth day of the eighth month, in the month <u>which he had devised in his own heart.</u>"** (1 Kin. 12:33)

We are warned that our hearts are deceitful above all things and we may not trust in them. This is why we so desperately need to stand on the solid rock, which is the Word of God for our direction and lifestyle. In the fourth century, another national leader devised a feast in his own heart. His name was Constantine and the feast is called Easter. How did God react to Jeroboam's little 'addition' to the cycle of divinely ordained feasts? Well, it was because of this idolatry that God punished the house of Israel and sent them into exile to become 'the lost ten tribes of Israel.'

> **"I will take away the remnant of the house of Jeroboam, as one takes away refuse until it is all gone...And He will give Israel** (not Judah) **up because of the sins of Jeroboam, who sinned and who made Israel sin."** (1 Kin. 14:10, 16)

God is Judge

We must keep in mind the history of Israel here; that the tribe of Yehudah (Judah) had separated from the rest of the tribes of Israel due to their rebellion against King Solomon's son, Rehoboam. The tribes of Israel persisted in idolatry and rebellion, for which God 'gave them up' and only preserved Judah to this day. Some believe that those re-gathered in the Messiah are actually of these 'lost' tribes of Israel who are only now forsaking their pagan ways and re-discovering their Israelite identity. Whether a remnant of the Church is actually from these cast off tribes of Israel or not (which I think is difficult to prove conclusively either way), the important matter is the forsaking of idolatrous practices and feasts that originate in the devising of a man's heart rather than the word of God – including Easter! Will God judge those who persist in celebrating Easter? I am very glad that this is not my job to decide, but only His who is perfectly righteous and also abundant in mercy.

I would like to include here an answer that I wrote on our website to someone wrestling with this very issue:

Questions and Answers:

Passover/Easter

Q: Hello from Astoria, Oregon! Ok I have questions, lots of questions. Our family has been invited (3rd year in a row) to a church party on Easter. The only easter tradition that is done is the egg hunt. The rest of the time we fellowship and play games and eat. There are about 40 to 50 people here and we really enjoy this time. (our church love whole church gatherings) Our Mother Church and our own church is learning about the Jewish Traditions. We keep the true sabbath. Our mother church and our church keep it on Sunday. I have thought about showing up after the hunt but that is always later on in the day. Do you have any suggestions. I love to be part of the crowd. I guess that eventually I will have to make a stand. I don't know of any good churches in our area. Our Pastor is young and knows the Spirit and follows. Some times I feel that God is just not leading him in this area right now. He is learning about the Sabbath now. That is a big step for him. He started out as a scare them to the Lord man. He is just now learning about patience and love (with people) I understand if your response takes time. My husband and I are praying about what to do on the 15th. I would also like to know more about what and how to follow the jewish ways.

A. Dear Sister, I can sense in your letter that you are sincere and truly want to follow God and walk in His ways, but it is tough when it's such an upstream swim and all the other fish are swimming the other way, calling out to you, "Hey!! You're going the wrong wayyyyyyyyyy!" My first impression was to tell you all about the paganism of Easter and send you some information, and tell you that if you don't get out of Babylon you will be swept away with her sins. (Rev. 18:4) But the Lord has showed me something, I believe, that is in line with the decision of the

Jerusalem council in Acts 15. That is, we should not be too hard on Gentiles who are turning from paganism to God's ways and Torah. In the beginning, it can seem overwhelming. We must learn line by line and precept upon precept. Although we should all be moving in the direction of obedience to God's word, it is difficult to change all at once everything in our lives. I would like to give the illustration through which God spoke to me:

Bowing in the House of Rimmon

Naaman, captain of the host of the king of Aram, was a mighty man but a leper. A little captive Jewish maid suggested he go to the prophet in Israel to find healing. He was instructed to wash seven times in the Jordan river to be cleansed of his leprosy. Naaman was angry. The rivers of Damascus, and other Gentile lands were far superior to Israel's Jordan river, he stated. But he was convinced to obey the prophet anyway and he came out of the river healed and cleansed. No longer leprous. Leprosy symbolized moral sin. The remedy for man's moral fallen condition is not found in seemingly superior waters of India, Greece, Rome, or any other land, but in the river of Hebraic, Biblical teachings from the Torah. Because of his healing, Naaman dedicated himself to the God of Israel, knowing him to be the one true God. But then he asks forgiveness (pardon). "In this thing the lord pardon thy servant; when my master goes into the House of Rimmon to worship there, and he leans on my hand, and I prostrate myself in the house of rimmon, when I prostrate myself in the House of Rimmon, the lord pardon thy servant in this thing.' And he (Elisha) said unto him; go in peace" (2 kings 5:18-19)

This phrase, "To bow in the house of Rimmon", has become an indication of unwilling homage, or dangerous compromise.

Some would say that everyone should be like Daniel, and rather than compromise their faith, be thrown into the lion's den, or like Shadrach, Meshach, and Abednego, and be thrown into the fire rather than compromise. But Naaman was a new believer, a baby in the faith as some would say. Elisha said, "Go in peace". He didn't say he approved, nor that he disapproved. I believe he was simply giving him leave and trusting the Lord to help him grow in faith and obedience. If Elisha had rebuked him for his 'bowing in the house of Rimmon', perhaps Naaman might have become discouraged and fallen away completely from his new turning to the One True God. And so I would also tend to say, go in peace, and I trust that yes, one day you will have the strength and courage to take a stand. Love Hannah

Falling Away

Added note: In the time since the first writing of this book, we have seen so many, many sincere Christians who become enamored with their 'Jewish roots' eventually come to a place of falling away from their faith. It begins innocently enough with some interest in exploring our common roots and to celebrate the Biblical feasts and the seventh day sabbath as well as keeping the Biblical food laws. Then it sometimes lead to an anti-Church, anti-Christian attitude. This causes some to abandon their assembling together with other Spirit -filled Believers who don't seem to understand them. Isolation sets the stage for deception and eventually they question everything about the Christian faith including Yeshua (Jesus) Himself.

This is a very real danger that I must, in all good conscience, warn readers against this practice. Our focus must always remain on the finished work of Yeshua (Jesus); on His love for us and ours for Him. It is all too easy to fall prey to the schemes of the enemy that we would lose our 'first love' if we are ignorant of this trap. So I plead with you to keep your wits about you as you move into your study and celebration of Passover and the other feasts and keep Yeshua (Jesus) always as the cornerstone.

CHAPTER SIXTEEN

A Call To Passover

I would like to close with one final biblical plea to join with us in celebrating Passover, and to ignore those who mock and ridicule you for doing so. King Hezekiah sent letters to all of Israel and Judah, exhorting them to come to the house of the Lord at Jerusalem to keep the Passover to the Lord God of Israel, since they had not done it for a long time in the prescribed manner. (2 Chron. 30:1-5) The runners went throughout the entire kingdom with the King's command,

> **"Children of Israel, return to the Lord God of Abraham, Isaac, and Israel; then He will return to the remnant of you who have escaped…Now do not be stiff-necked as your father were, but yield yourselves to the Lord…for the Lord your God is gracious and merciful, and will not turn His face from you if you return to Him."** (2 Chron. 30: 6, 8-9)

But what were some of the people's reaction?

> **"They laughed at them and mocked them."**
> (2 Chron. 30:10)

And yet God gave some singleness of heart to obey the command of the king and the leaders, at the word of the Lord. And a very great assembly gathered to keep the Feast of Unleavened Bread (v.12-13). The people feasted and rejoiced before the Lord even beyond the required seven days for another seven days! Such was the joy they experienced in re-dedicating themselves to the Lord through keeping the Feast.

> **"And their prayers came up to His holy dwelling place, to heaven."** (2 Chron. 30: 27)

May you also experience great joy and renewed strength in the Lord as you return to a celebration of His appointed times (moadim), Passover and First Fruits.

Isaiah 53

Surely he took up our infirmities and carried our sorrows, yet we considered him stricken by God, smitten by him, and afflicted. But he was pierced for our transgressions, he was crushed for our iniquities; the punishment that brought us peace was upon him, and by his wounds we are healed. We all, like sheep, have gone astray, each of us has turned to his own way; and the LORD has laid on him the iniquity of us all.

He was oppressed and afflicted, yet he did not open his mouth; he was led like a lamb to the slaughter, and as a sheep before her shearers is silent, so he did not open his mouth. By oppression and judgment he was taken away. And who can speak of his descendants? For he was cut off from the land of the living; for the transgression of my people he was stricken. He was assigned a grave with the wicked, and with the rich in his death, though he had done no violence, nor was any deceit in his mouth.

Yet it was the LORD'S will to crush him and cause him to suffer, and though the LORD makes his life a guilt offering, he will see his offspring and prolong his days, and the will of the LORD will prosper in his hand. After the suffering of his soul, he will see the light of life, and be satisfied; by his knowledge my righteous servant will justify many, and he will bear their iniquities. Therefore I will give him a portion among the great, and he will divide the spoils with the strong, because he poured out his life unto death, and was numbered with the transgressors. For he bore the sin of many, and made intercession for the transgressors.

Isaiah 53:4-12 (NIV)

CHAPTER SEVENTEEN

FINAL PRAYER

If you are not absolutely certain that you would be covered by the blood of the Passover Lamb, Yeshua the Messiah, please pray from your heart,

> "God of my fathers, Avraham, Yitzchak and Yaacov, I accept and receive the sacrifice of Yeshua (Jesus), Your Son, as my Passover Lamb. Please forgive my sins through His blood of atonement and cover me with His blood in order that your wrath will not destroy me, but that You would see the blood and pass over me. Thank you that Your power raised Yeshua from the dead and that through my faith in Him, I will also follow Him into eternal life. Please make me a new creation; reveal to me Your purpose for my life and help me to fulfill it. Thank you that You will never leave me or forsake me. Amen."

APPENDIX

Recipes

Baba's Passover Rolls

½ cup oil
2 cups matza meal
½ tsp salt
2 cups boiling water
1 tbsp sugar
4 eggs
2 tbsp potato starch

Add oil to boiling water in a pan on top of the stove. Add dry ingredients all at once. Beat rapidly over low heat until mix leaves sides of pan. Remove from heat. Beat eggs separately and fold in beaten eggs into mix. Beat until hard and smooth. Shape into balls and bake on greased baking sheet @400 degrees for 1 hour or until golden brown. Serve warm and eat with butter and honey or jam.

Passover Fudge Brownies

2 ½ bars (3 ½ oz.) bittersweet chocolate
¼ cup oil or butter
2 eggs
1/8 tsp salt
2/3 cup sugar
½ cup cake meal
½ cup coarsely chopped walnuts

Melt chocolate and butter over hot water. Cool. Beat eggs and salt until thick and lemon colored. Gradually beat in sugar. Beat in cooled chocolate mix. Gradually add cake meal and beat until well blended. Stir in chopped nuts. Spread batter evenly in well greased 8" square pan. Bake 350 degrees for 30 min. or until done. Cut while hot and let cool in pan.

To contact the Author write:

Hannah Nesher, Voice for Israel
Suite #313- 11007 Jasper Ave.
Edmonton, Alberta
T5K 0K6 Canada

www.voiceforisrael.net

Please include your testimony or help received from this book when you write. Your prayer requests are welcome

Hannah is also available for speaking engagements. Please contact through the website or e-mail:
nesher.hannah@gmail.com

Additional Teaching Materials by Hannah Nesher

DVDs

Shalom Morah I (Hebrew for Christians & Hebrew Names of God) 11 DVD set
Shalom Morah II (Hebrew for Christians & Wisdom in the Hebrew Alphabet) 10 DVD set
Exploring the Jewish Roots of the Christian Faith
Unity in the Messiah
Because He Lives
Messianic Jewish Wedding in Jerusalem
There is a God in Israel
Messianic Jewish Passover
Passover Lamb or Easter Ham?
Voice Out of Zion II (Where is Your Brother Jacob?) Walking Through the Wilderness
Ruth: A Righteous Gentile
Messiah in Chanukah
Blow the Shofar in Zion

BOOKS

Grafted in Again
Journey to Jerusalem
Come Out of Her My People
Messiah Revealed in Purim
Messiah Revealed in the Sabbath
Messiah Revealed in the Fall Feasts
Messiah Revealed in Chanukah
Kashrut: The Biblical Dietary Laws
Messiah Revealed in Shavuot
You Know My Heart (English booklet)
You Know My Heart (Hebrew booklet)

If you enjoyed this book and would like to learn more, don't miss the companion DVDs

PASSOVER LAMB OR EASTER HAM?

Over the centuries the Church has strayed from its roots and the 'Passover Lamb' has become an 'Easter Ham', declared by God as unclean and not fit for holy people! Join us for a Spirit-filled Passover in this teaching by a Messianic Jewish-Israeli Bible teacher and be set free from the pagan influences the Church has adopted by error.

MESSIANIC JEWISH PASSOVER

Join a Messianic Jewish Israeli woman as she guides a congregation through a Passover Seder. Drawing upon her experiences in the traditional Jewish Passover and her faith in Messiah Yeshua (Jesus), this teaching glorifies Jesus as the Lamb of God, who was slain for our sins.

Hannah Nesher, Voice for Israel
Suite #313- 11007 Jasper Ave.
Edmonton, Alberta
T5K 0K6 Canada

www.voiceforisrael.net

www.ingramcontent.com/pod-product-compliance
Lightning Source LLC
LaVergne TN
LVHW051603070426
835507LV00021B/2745